T0274675

ADVANCE PRAISE

"Powerful and moving. Make this book your friend. It gives wise and insightful counsel, and is bursting with love for the natural world. I will be returning often to its pages."

ARIANNA HUFFINGTON,

FOUNDER & CEO, THRIVE GLOBAL

"A profound guide to discovering the great wisdom in the natural world, this book by James Thornton is a treasure for all."

ROSHI JOAN HALIFAX,

ABBOT, UPAYA ZEN CENTER

"James Thornton is an environmental hero of the highest order. James's extraordinary book *Nature, My Teacher* is captivating, mesmerising, and manages to capture so beautifully our true relationship with the natural world. This is a hugely important book."

BEN GOLDSMITH,

AUTHOR OF *GOD IS AN OCTOPUS*

"This is a beautiful, important and uplifting book. In it James Thornton lays out his love for the planet in a way that is thought-provoking and lyrical, a spacious blend of prose and poetry flavoured with the subtleties of the author's Zen training. I came away inspired by the wisdom I had encountered in these pages and by the unmistakable aftertaste of compassion."

ANTONY OSLER,

AUTHOR OF *STOEP ZEN*

"This marvellous, poetic collection of insights is full of humility, wisdom and wonder. Some are satirical, some joyous, some uncomfortably challenging and some just plain sad. But weaving through all of them is Thornton's irrepressible faith in humankind. 'Help me do something about it', he says, when writing about the dwindling of the natural world. And then he offers a beautiful roadmap for how we can find the resources inside ourselves to do just that. Unmissable."

GABRIELLE WALKER,

AUTHOR OF *ANTARCTICA*

JAMES THORNTON is a Zen Buddhist priest, and Founder and President of ClientEarth, the leading global non-profit environmental law group. *The New Statesman* named him as one of ten people who could change the world. A poet, essayist and novelist, James is the co-author of *Client Earth* (Scribe 2018), which won the Judges' Selection, Business Book of the Year in the UK and the Green Book of the Year from Santa Monica Libraries in the US. He has three times won Leader of the Year at the Business Green Awards. For his legal work, *The Financial Times* awarded him its Lifetime Achievement Award. He is a Member of the China Council for International Cooperation on Environment and Development, and Honorary Professor of Law at the University of Bristol. He studied philosophy at Yale and got his Juris Doctor at New York University Law School, where he was editor-in-chief of the Law Review. He was Executive Director of the Heffter Institute, a neuroscience institute that pioneered the study of psychotropic molecules. He lives in Los Angeles and London.

Nature,
My
Teacher

JAMES THORNTON

BARB
ICAN
PRESS

Published by Barbican Press, Los Angeles and London
Copyright © James Thornton, 2024

This book is copyright under the Berne Convention. No
reproduction without permission. All rights reserved.

The right of James Thornton to be identified as the author of this book
has been asserted by him in accordance with sections 77 and 78 of the
Copyright, Designs and Patents Act, 1988.

Registered UK office: 1 Ashenden Road, London E5 0DP
US office: 1032 19th Street, Unit 2, Santa Monica CA90403

www.barbicanpress.com
@barbicanpress1

Library of Congress Control Number: 2023945431

A CIP catalogue for this book is available from the British Library

Typeset by Tetragon, London
Distributed in North America by Publishers Group West

ISBN: 978-1-909954-93-9

Also by James Thornton

For Taizan Maezumi Roshi
my beloved Zen teacher

Contents

To be truly radical is to make hope possible
rather than despair convincing

RAYMOND WILLIAMS

Introduction

I met Montaigne in my teens and never forgot. His reason and rambles have moved writers ever since he sharpened a quill in his tower in the 16th century.

He said his essays were about himself. He asked 'what do I know?' He coined the word 'essay' for the literary form we grew up with. His essays were philosophical assays, attempts to capture a thought, an idea, turn it around, apply it to his life. His intimate disclosure of self was a radical invention. He was criticized for it, but his essays changed the world of self-expression.

My book of essays is about myself too. Since I understand myself to include the living world, the essays touch on the state of the wider living world. The essays pick up from Montaigne's question 'what do I know?' by asking 'who am I?' What is the nature of self in the world in which it appears?

In this sequence of essays, I take the Earth as my school and Nature as my teacher.

The Book of Nature

Nature is my teacher

By then I'd been studying with my Zen teacher Maezumi Roshi many years. We were up in the San Jacinto Mountains at his mountain center, near the ridge top. I could hike up, find blooming lupine bushes swarming with bumble bees, and look out over the desert far below toward Palm Springs.

Martin was picking me up at the end of a long meditation retreat. He had never met Maezumi, and it was time. I arranged for them to have a private word.

Martin told Maezumi that his own practice was to go to mountains and experience the sacred. He asked Maezumi if he felt the same way about mountains. Maezumi said that of course he did. Even his name meant Big Mountain. He invited Martin to come walk the mountains next time I was there meditating on my cushion.

Then Martin thanked Maezumi.

"Thank you for the teachings you have given James all these years. They are very important to him."

"I am not James's teacher!" thundered Maezumi. "Nature! Nature is *his* teacher!"

Waking

Waking, I remember small things and move up in scale. Quantum foam to living cells to earwig mothers caring for their young then black holes stealing information away from space.

It's like falling in love with a person. I'm enshrouded in mystery, want to know more, am sustained by quiet joy.

Humbled too. I want to know everything but can never know everything. To hold onto something fixed and solid but there is nothing fixed and solid. Unknowns extend in all directions to be chased with passion and questions.

Whatever time I have will allow me to perceive, reflect on and praise the smallest part of it.

How to proceed?

Reason is my ball of string in the minotaur's labyrinth. Heart impels me forward.

My voyages of discovery show this project has no boundaries.

I learn it is my religion.

The butcherbird has the better part

In California's San Jacinto mountains I sit down before dawn to meditate then stay through heat of day. My meditation is to listen, really listen. Dawn light gives single tribes of bird the soundscape in their turns. As light rises the different tribes join into ensemble. Later morning warmth brings insects to complete the work. Nature music, its shared ecosystem of sound, fills me then and stays, lives inside me vivid.

Later in a concert hall I listen to musicians play against an Australian butcherbird on tape. I'm there because I miss the butcher's song, last heard at Uluru, amplified by memory. The butcher on tape spins out his sexy taunting line: Come to me baby, stay away boys. It has the better part.

Nature's musicians are beyond us.

What if you slow down the butcher's song, slow it down way down? Will it sound like whale song? If you speed up a whale song's slow cadence will it sound like bird song? Another song of here I am and where are you? Of vigor advertised. Of virtuosity underlining virility. Of longing and reflection.

When you go deep as forest understorey, deep like a sea trench is deep, are we all singing different parts in one song, not metaphorically but really?

Chinese flower

In the world of plants a fritillary's a lily who hangs its blooms like lanterns. *Fritillaria delavayi* grows alpine in west China to forty-seven hundred meters. Its life on scree is slow. Five years to flower then a single yellow bloom each June onward.

People come to disturb its peace, seeking ingredients for remedies. The lily bulb removes heat they think, moistens the lung, resolves phlegm and relieves coughs. Prices are up in recent years with picking intensified so the fritillary has quietly taken action.

Scientists from Kunming Institute of Botany found where picking is high, fritillaries have camouflaged themselves, evolving from green leaves with yellow flowers to brown flowers with brown leaves. Experiments show brown flowers against scree are harder for human eyes to find.

This lily becomes the first wild plant we know wily enough to don camouflage against us. Though others may be hiding.

Insects were

Mourn those virtuosos of diversity. Remember in summer your parents would drive then had to clean windscreen and headlights of bodies the car's hurtling crushed to small death. No more. German entomologists collected flying insects in traps and weighed them over decades. Now the numbers are three quarters down even in nature reserves. It's the pesticides in surrounding lands, they think.

Still I hoped for plenitude in tropical forest. Today a study shows insects have plummeted in pristine Puerto Rican rainforest the same way. Here it might be global heating pushing the male reproductive systems beyond limits. Tropical forest birds and others who depend on them are also down. Flowers and trees will follow.

I knew we'd lose a lot of birds and mammals during my lifetime but consoled myself with insects. I hadn't realized they would go too during my watch.

But we can make repairs. For the tropics, arrest global heating and let evolution move toward a cadre that can bear the new norm. For the rest, throw away the poisons. Insects will rebound. With them the mountainous life that builds on them. There's no need to say insects were. Not yet.

Mediterranean Spring

Serins are the sound of the Mediterranean in Springtime, my forty-two-year-old field guide tells me. Close relatives of the wild canary, the yellow male sits high in a bush or tree to sing.

What is the nature of his song, how describe his sound.

Words don't have enough hands, don't have fingers enough to touch the shapes of melody as they move through time nor grasp then mold them into transmissible tokens.

So you need meetings with serins.

Generations of serins have passed since they first agreed to meet me. In recent years none came by. I've awaited their return, their tribe dwindling. This spring they're back in strong voice.

Their melodies are dense and fast.

We hear clumsy, scientists found, a rushed and garbled version of what unfolds for them. Songs spread out in pitch and time when a bird listens and rhythm opens too.

The serins' return feels a reprieve and their reach into realms where I can't follow opens a space of appreciation, fashioned from my limits.

Voice of the valley

You stand at the head of the valley. The voice of the wind emerges by touching things. Stones, leaves, flanks of hills. The voice comes soft as a light breeze, then builds. Leaves, mostly it's leaves moving side to side. In the distance you see them move, waves on an ocean, on a wheat field. When shaking in storm, a million hands wave angry.

The sound percusses and you perceive. Listen to green summer leaves their sound mapping onto air to your ears their growth, water into roots up trunk into shapes where chlorophyll makes sugars feeding life.

Recently a different note entered, a drier timbre as hot winds from Africa cross the waters with desiccant affinities. The forest sounds like autumn though the calendar says late spring while birds still raise their young.

You connect this forest tone of voice with global patterns and wonder how long the forest will endure how long will we. Looking out one day and listening, words come to your mind. What you hear is this. The verdure endures, not you.

CLIENT VISIT

At the tip of Africa, the Agulhas Plain, on a twenty-eight thou-sand hectare reserve.

No motors mar the soundscape, nor human works the landscape.

Martin and our guide are with me. My other companions: blue cranes, hippo, wildebeest, three kinds of kingfisher, three of flycatcher, many more.

The abundance of life here raises a quiet rejoicing. I'm visiting my Client.

Listening to friends

I'm on my balcony in the fynbos, practicing unapologetic rest, when a cricket's song suggests I listen to my friends. A bird pipes up who sings behind a wall. It's a southern boubou, a kind of bushshrike. I listen for half an hour.

She dialogues with herself, by turns gleeful, squawky, kvetchy, doubtful, chortling, angry, tuneful. A soliloquy on her week nattered in low voice, no one else to hear.

When her song ends, its absence gives me the mountain's silence.

Summit with baboons

I sit on the stoop. Rain falls on the fynbos. Raucous toads call. As I consider how to use the rest of my life, arthritis troubles my right hand.

This morning we walked up the mountain. A family of baboons surmounted the summit from the other side. Seeing us the male barked loud. We did not dispute his claim or further intrude.

Day's end

Sunset on this mountain. A dove calls, a hundred swallows flash by, blue headed lizard does push ups, a squadron of hadada ibis squawk.

None of them have contributed to climate change.

Although the full moon will rise soon, not one of them needs to make atonement.

Blackbird syntax

A column In Praise of Springtime said, "The song of the Blackbird is, of course, a cliché".

The song of the Blackbird is a cliché said the writer, said the column, said the Guardian, a *cliché*. Decades later the mud of these words remain.

Was the writer's head full of ghosts telling him not to feel the song. Did he love but feel a need to betray. Like Judas.

Raising our heads, what about the song?

Blackbird's song stakes out territory good for breeding. Blackbird's song asks her to say yes to the next generation of Blackbirds. Blackbird's song is life's message in real time. Blackbird's song is evolving in our noise, to carry above machines.

Since songbirds' brains are better at sound, Blackbird's song enfolds more music than we can hear. Let alone penetrate the syntax of their life.

We can rip through the curtain though. To hear the boulevardier in every Blackbird singing. To hear the seductive dinosaur in every Blackbird song.

We are offered richness beyond our reckoning every time we hear the Blackbird's song, even when his soundstage is the TV antenna on a broken-down house.

To an audience in a hall in Yorkshire I read a poem aloud, singing praise for Blackbirds. As I read, a Blackbird joins from outside, singing full-throated to the sky, concluding his run as I read out my last word.

A cliché, you say?

Sunset for parasites

It was beetles. We thought there were more species of beetles than of any other creature.

Asked to say something about God, atheist JBS Haldane said He had an inordinate fondness for beetles. Their diversity is easy to see across the natural world. Handsome, easily collected, filling museum cases with form and pattern, color and iridescence. More beetles are named as species than any other order of animal.

Wasps are harder to see and to love, more dangerous and delicate, tiny parasitic ones especially. Their parasite lifestyle leads direct to diversity. A wasp can set up shop as a beetle's parasite. One on each different species of beetle. One on every species of beetle. The same for butterflies, each species' caterpillar exposed to mother wasp's needle, laying her eggs to hatch and eat the caterpillar from inside out. Other wasps are fair game too, even other parasitic ones, a cascade of exponential parasitism. Each upward level of wasp smaller and harder to see to collect to name and so admire.

Wasps are simply the best of all the Animalia at parasitism. So it's wasps over beetles as the most speciose animal order, maybe three times as numerous, many still unknown.

Getting to know them would have been a satisfying lifework in less perilous times. To specialize as they do makes wasps vulnerable, of course. When we extinguish species it's sunset for their obligate parasites.

Death cap

Mushrooms with purest poison offer innocuous smiles. Twice I've read of mycologists, professional mushroom men, picking and eating ones that fooled then killed them. In Poland at mushroom time when old people offered wild mushrooms for sale along the forest road, we drove on at my request.

We seldom think of fungi, like most important things. Respect arrives when we learn their subtle threads link forest, field, crops and countries and the fabric of our life depends on theirs. Poisonous mushrooms, who've contrived a cabinet of toxins, call for special attention. Some interfere with RNA to cause cell death. Who were they fending off? Deer and badger, triceratops and stegosaur? Their dangerous arts are older than us.

Then come the names of mushrooms. Some alluring, some warning, some sticking in memory like an old flame. Under broad leaves of oak and beech grows Death Cap, attracting many. Then Destroying Angel—eat a bit then liver and kidneys collapse slowly without cure. These two take the greatest toll.

There's Paralysis Funnel, moved up from Morocco to France and Italy and looks esculent to the locals, with neurotoxic effect. Funeral Bells, increasingly common on bark mulch in gardens, and Veiled Poison Pie, the discreet member of the poison pie family. Surprise Webcap, which lets you know hours later. The Silencer and Devil's Bolete are tempting.

Wouldn't you choose the Fenugreek Milkcap or Fruity Firecap from the tasting menu? The Mousepee Pinkgill politely warns you off, while the Blushing Dapperling flirts. And the winsome Grisette pulls you in like that old romance, the one that returns in dreams. But it's so easily confused with Death Cap it could lead to murder.

Thirty-Ton Americans

In my seafood restaurant on the Santa Cruz pier, I sit with a view of the ocean and a glass of wine. I read about a new metabolic theory of ecology. It's a beauty.

There have been no good general theories in ecology until this one. It says that as your body mass increases, your resource use goes up too, but more slowly. So a moose weighs ten thousand times more than a mouse, but eats only one thousand times more. Each gram of mouse tissue uses energy ten times faster than a gram of moose tissue, and the mouse's heart beats ten times faster than the moose's heart. The moose lives ten times longer but also has a gestation period ten times longer.

I start in on my oysters. Each dab of soft pearly flesh concentrates the perfume of the sea. A dozen go down before I know it. Mollified, I go back to the theory. What I like best is the way it points up how special we humans are.

Every other primate—indeed every other organism—fits into the same pattern of metabolism, growth, reproduction and energy consumption. Alone in the history of life we stand out. We don't stand out just a little. We jut out as Mount Everest would in the middle of the Sahara.

Other animals consume energy only in food. We go beyond mere dining. We suck down energy from ancient biological sources in oil, gas and coal along with our daily bread.

When you look at our energy metabolism, humans in the first world are colossi. To be exact, each American consumes energy like a thirty-ton primate. We are each King or Queen Kong.

Before we learned to guzzle oil, humans weighed only what the bathroom scale said. Women often had ten children. The theory, though, spells out how fertility goes down as size goes up. The theory says that a thirty-ton American female should have slightly less than two offspring in her lifetime, just what we see happening.

Meanwhile, the first oysters were so good I've ordered another dozen. As I let one of the little creatures slide down my throat, I consider what it means to be a thirty-ton primate.

Seen in this revealing light, your average American is by far the largest land mammal in the history of life. The previous record holder, an extinct rhino called *Indiothermium,* wasn't even close. It weighed in at a paltry ten tons, only a third of our metabolic bulk.

The largest land mammal today is the African bull elephant, a mere six tons. *Tyrannosaurus rex,* surprisingly puny at five tons, shrinks in impotent fear before today's thirty-ton American.

Our only competition is the blue whale at a hundred and thirty tons. But don't be daunted. Put its bulk in perspective. First, the blue whale is supported by water, an unfair advantage. Second, the highest population that blue whales ever achieved was just two hundred thousand in all the world's oceans. We've culled them down to a more manageable ten thousand by now. Even at their peak, the blue whale population was spread thin. For comparison, two hundred thousand is the population of Lubbock, Texas, which, though it lays claim to "an excellent business climate", is not one of our major conurbations.

Your average family of four going down to Walmart weighs in as the metabolic equivalent of a blue whale. We are majestic indeed.

I order a third dozen oysters because they're rather small and I have plenty of room. My mind turns to the primates in the European Union. They are something of a challenge to Americans. When you look at their energy use and discount the ten new and mostly poor Eastern European member states, Europeans bulk up to about twenty-five tons each. They're not as sumptuous as we, but they are players.

Meanwhile on the other continents, there's hunger and longing. Everyone wants to consume as much as the average American. Who can blame them? Everyone wants to become a thirty-ton primate. Nor can any reasonable person argue that life, liberty and the pursuit of happiness—which we can now quantify as thirty metabolic tons—should be denied to these less fortunate people.

On the pier in Santa Cruz, I tuck into my main course. I add more tartar sauce to my succulent 'captain's catch'. Chewing, I start to imagine the world of the future. I picture a socially just world in which we manage to give everyone in the Developing World as much energy to consume as everyone in the first world now has.

I become entranced with this vision. Imagine what this future will be like. Imagine ten billion humans, each of them thirty tons, bestriding the planet. Can the rule of the dinosaurs offer anything as thrilling? Ten billion thirty-ton primates stomping around in work and pleasure! The very plains tremble, the very mountains shake! When we dance the very oceans spill over like water from a hand basin! What can stop us now?

Calling for more wine with my dessert, I look up. The late sun gilds everyone on the Santa Cruz pier. Comfortable couples walk. They refresh themselves, dipping into bags of fried food, or licking jumbo ice creams. Most of them, old and young alike, have guts hanging over their belts like mudslides. Good people enjoying their access to energy.

I finish my pie, drink the last of my wine, walk back along the pier to my hotel. I see two swimmers in the twilight. They seem too small for people. When my eyes resolve them, I see they are sea otters. A mother and pup.

The mother swims under the pier, disappearing down into dark emerald water. She is gathering mussels. Appearing again, she backstrokes to her babe while crunching the shells loud.

They meet and nuzzle, then the mother gives part of the catch over to be crunched in turn. It is an easy, lazy life. But then, I reflect, the baby weighs practically nothing. Even the mother otter would barely make a dinner portion. It's easy to keep such a modest metabolism stoked on mussels.

As I walk off the pier a prosperous couple in their late thirties asks me if they can drive onto the pier to get to their dinner spot. I say they can drive, but might want to walk, since they could see a mother otter feeding her baby.

"Wonderful," says the man, "but we've already seen them in the aquarium!" They jump back in their Mercedes and drive onto the pier for dinner. Arriving by Mercedes is easier than walking when you are thirty tons.

STILL CHEWING

Next morning and I'm still chewing over the metabolic theory that led me to understand the truly colossal size of each and every American consumer. I begin to wonder if this theory doesn't explain the rest of human history too.

Perhaps Caesar can be understood as having co-opted the metabolism of his legions. If each of Caesar's soldiers weighed in at a hundred and fifty pounds, generous given their small stature, it would take only four hundred men under his control to raise Caesar to the magic metabolic weight of thirty tons. Since he had more like ten thousand men rampaging through Gaul with him, Caesar's true size was more like seven hundred and fifty tons, an awesome mammal.

It becomes clear why Caesar, with a weight like that, cut such a wide swathe in history. Alexander the Great, Genghis Khan and history's other great men co-opted armies of energy-users to further their careers. Their own metabolic sizes thus blossomed so much that they too became even greater than today's average American, thus towering above their contemporaries.

Metabolic size matters.

MISS GRAY

Alice Gray opened the door of Nature for me.

She was in her fifties and an entomologist at the American Museum of Natural History in New York. Her office occupied a whole floor of the Museum's grand southern tower overlooking Central Park.

I was ten and had gone to meet her to get a tarantula. In those days, tarantulas were unavailable in pet shops, and all paths led to Miss Gray.

After taking my tarantula home I went back to visit Miss Gray as often as I could. I had imprinted on her like a baby duck on its mother.

She invited me to join the Junior Entomological Society, an offshoot of the august American Entomological Society, whose scientist members met at the Museum.

One day on an entomology field trip, I lamented that insect pests and parasites messed things up. So Miss Gray told me a story.

When she was a girl, her mother grew vegetables in their garden in Connecticut. One day Alice was out in the garden. To her horror she saw the potato crop was being destroyed by an infestation of the voracious Colorado Potato Beetle, a gemlike bug in black and gold.

Alice ran in and sounded the alarm to her mother. Her mother with great calm replied, yes Alice, we'll lose all the potatoes, but look at what beautiful beetles we have!

About four years later, my family was moving from New York to South Bend, Indiana. A decision was made that I could take my tarantulas and scorpions, as long as I held them in boxes in my lap on the car trip, which was fine by me.

But I would have to leave behind Smedley, my fine chameleon from Madagascar, who had eyes on swivels. Naturally I took him to Miss Gray to live in her tower.

When I next visited New York, I rushed in to see Miss Gray.

She said, I have sad news for you. Poor Smedley is dead. But upon his death, the most beautiful parasitic wasp bored a hole and emerged from his corpse!

Which contented us both.

Remember when

remember when   you were   floating through slime
your single cell guided   to engulf   particles   of food
by a sense   like smell

remember when   you wriggled   nerve cord now stretching
head to tail   as you navigated   the sea floor

remember when   your backbone   appeared   and let
your strong fins   flicker fast
through darting shoals

remember when   sound   first blossomed
and you crawled   onto land   before
trees were born

remember when   sight opened   and you
could see her   feel her   touch her   taste her

remember when   you first played
in this ape body   first sang
first loved   first realized

The Book of Self
and Other

Biggest heart

A blue whale in the womb listens to her mother's heart and hears deeper rhythms than our own. Gentle in its vastness, the blue whale eats krill. Diving, its huge heart slows down to two beats a minute. Its heart is the most generously proportioned in life's long history: the size of a sofa you could curl up on.

Approaching by boat, coming close, you see only a little blue island with a blowhole as the whale rests at the surface. You enter the presence of a master and it changes you. You enter clarity and see vast space in your mind's eye. Powerful compassion enters you along with peace.

On our boat a ten-year-old boy sat quiet with everyone else, felt the whale, then tears came to him and took him.

Young man in the photo

He draws your eye. Cheeks, neck and belly all slim, with a grace that pulls you to him, standing in a Hanoi market, turned to the side, looking at a stall. He'll fill out in time under the influence of age and gravity and migrate to the background.

Thickness inside builds slowly. The dead skin of disappointment, cuticle of envy, impermeable layers of irritation accrete and obscure. They become old glass with poor optical quality. In the end you fail to see the world outside. Smooth the accretions away as they build, using the emotional equivalents of grater, parer and kitchen knife, and the view clears.

When my aunt Alice was eighty-four, she told me "there are only two kinds of old women: those who've become very nice and those who are nasty."

Swash and backwash

Swash and backwash as sea strokes shore accreting and eroding. What falls into the swash and backwash falls away. What falls away is the pain of the heart tight from hours on the screen so you nearly scream though you want to smile and try to smile. What falls away is the repetitive worry sown by evidence that some who claim friendship are enemies. Though you know your enemy is your teacher the one who shows the path to patience though you know this and try to be grateful for your enemies' help along the path it is hard to recall hard to be grateful when you are dodging cars and putting in long hours in polluted cities.

What falls away falls into the sea while a blackbird sings his song older than all of us. The blackbird sings by a church being rethatched for the hundredth time in its long career. His song floats above the chirruping of sparrows above the wails of gulls above the cries of children above the swash and backwash.

What falls away falls away and opens into an appreciation though partial always partial and necessarily partial an appreciation of the sweep of causes that led to this moment and this falling away this grateful moment.

My father's outrage

My father was outraged by the idea of original sin. That a baby is born swaddled in sin. That sin could be assigned before volition could occur. Where did the idea come from—is it to explain why we harm: the cruelty of demagogues, the cheating of my neighbor and the violence in my heart?

The myth of apple and serpent seems naïve now, like tribes who believed the Sun is a gourd hanging high in the sky. Greed, anger and ignorance, though, remain a vivid part of me. My inner violence has a rich range of shapes and intentions. In my origin story they're not born of original sin though. They're evolution's residue: how to survive, how to spot betrayal and betray in turn, how to steal a sexual encounter, how to dominate. My body knows these behaviors, my speech is quick with them, my mind ready to drive any advantage. These tendencies are my inheritance from the survival skills that made us both cooperative and vicious.

Nothing wrong with being aggressive meat eating apes. Children are not born into sin though. We are born with a toolbox we need to grow beyond. There are tools for that too.

In a fog I met a man

for Olafur Eliasson

In a fog I met a man. How did the fog arise. No need to know. Maybe warm air riding a glacier I was walking on. Maybe losing direction in midlife as Dante does at the beginning of his poem. Maybe the grief of my lost childhood. Of my wife. Of my lover. Of democracy in my country. Of the safe future for the biosphere that every generation took for granted and we cannot any longer. In the tunnel of my fog I can't tell time. Fog closes and opens. The sense of time is lost. I can't tell distance. All reference is gone. I wonder if I can tell taste from sight. If I can remember the basic coordinates of my internal compass. Why am I alive. What purpose does my life serve. What is my devotion. Who am I. Yet I keep moving in the invisible. Motion is required. Otherwise I would fall into the abyss and my deep program knows and so keeps me moving. Yet moving where. Moving how. And still moving. So there comes in the unknowing there comes something. Call it what. Call it trust. Accepting the unknowing. In the unknowing surrendering and dedicating myself. To whom. To all living things. In this fog then in this fog I met a man and who was he but this man I am becoming.

Weeds of doubt

A gentle rain sounds like new beginnings. Renewing an old friendship brings grounding. Waking up quietly offers change in the right direction. Nurturing the next generations brings purpose. Melding in marriage extends oneself. Pulling weeds of doubt brings deeper resonance. Working for the benefit of others instills meaning. Making oneself sustainable gives balance. All openings move us into the future with alacrity.

The way a gentle rain sounds like new beginnings. The way renewing an old friendship brings grounding. The way waking up quietly offers change in the right direction. The way nurturing the next generations brings purpose. The way melding in marriage extends oneself. The way pulling weeds of doubt brings deeper resonance. The way working for the benefit of others instills meaning. The way making oneself sustainable gives balance. The way all openings move us into the future with alacrity.

A gentle rain sounds like new beginnings. The way I hear it. Renewing an old friendship brings grounding. The way I feel it. Waking up quietly offers change in the right direction. The lift it gives me. Nurturing the next generation brings purpose. What I see as people age. Melding in marriage extends oneself. The way I learn. Pulling weeds of doubt brings deeper resonance. The way I tame my mind. Working for the benefit of others instills meaning. How I find hope. Making oneself sustainable gives balance. My incomplete project. All openings move us into the future with alacrity. How could I not be grateful.

What I tell myself today

The door is not a door to the fly, the TV not a source of news to the cat, the commuter rush of no concern to the dove. Subtler when you move to people but your music is noise to me, your honeypie doesn't move me, your dreams are foolish to me. When we come to ourself still subtler. What amused me yesterday doesn't today, if I'm drunk I'm unreliable, when I'm sick my perceptions shift. Socrates asked if he was the same man well and sick, fingering the fluidity.

This shifting self I cherish is a software program running in my wetware, shaped by evolution and vital for the organism's business. The self's not there in my earliest years, isn't in dreams or when I'm in the flow and won't be when I've got dementia. It comes and goes. No fixed thing. To know myself is to know the normal reactions of my program and see it's a program. Nothing that doesn't dissolve when you push on it.

The self that grows in the baby's brain and we know as adults shifts like a cloud. What is born and what dies is a trajectory. As the sutra has it, there is birth and death, there is also no birth and no death. Not the way we think of it. Not the way we fear it. What I tell myself today.

Meadow

Pneumonia recovery walk on my own, till friends come: soft-winged flower beetles in bindweed, speckled wood butterfly, tattered.

In the meadow a mother pushes her child in a stroller, bulldog trotting behind. The woman's smile suggests deep contentment and I realize how lucky she is.

I push through the meadow on an edge of understanding, aiming myself deeper. We're both having good days.

Liminal

There's a liminal side of being ill. Your boundary is softer its edges more open like the pores that open underneath when a leaf breathes. Your covering layer lies more porous against another. The mist lifts. The story of the other penetrates deeper and you follow into its forests its deserts its seamounts. You listen.

Their story allowed to enter. Their images their language. Not comparing not judging not testing for similarities for difference. Not running the subtle program in your mind that displays your own achievement or pain, insight or goals as more valuable more interesting more important than theirs. You hear.

Feeling the depth of the other the wholeness. Knowing the panorama of their journey is epic too and their time in this school of Earth as complex and valued as your own.

Last speaker

When I die my language will go with me. It's the same for you.
You are the last speaker of your language. When each of us goes
an entire universe will be extinguished.

What's wonderful is there's overlap enough between our universes
to let us communicate

before they dissolve.

Residing in the overlap, I look for moments.

Do something

A slow crimping happens when the morning sound you hear is motorcycle not dawn chorus. When diesel engines hound you as you walk and your lungs can't get fresh air. When planes drone over as you dodge hot fumes from buses. When you reach out through the noise and by a constructive act of imagination recall clear wind singing on the mountain and stars rising over the horned owl call.

There's a growing urgency in the loss. Knowing we are raking our planet clean of life. A deepening sadness from knowing the details of the dying. The species cut the forest cut the reef bleached. The songs of all the things that sing are being silenced. They jammed the music of our evolution and will guide it no more. As a loved one lays dying the wonder of life is clear.

Trivia like ego and entertainment and the social whirl fall away as a loved one lies dying. It's like that with the dwindling of the living world. The depth of sadness is a measure of love. The loss accretes. It is real and speeding. Everything every day brings it to me. This loss is the canvas on which everything appears. This sadness the background to all other feeling. Help me do something about it. Don't try to jolly me.

Care for them

Jared Diamond tells of decades spent with tribal people in New Guinea. There you live in small groups, a few dozen, he says. Your territory ringed by similar groups. You know them and exchange killings in a sustainable way. You killed my sister-in-law and now I kill your brother-in-law. Intimate tit for tat murders with spears and arrows.

Beyond this circle you don't know them or they you. If you venture there you kill any of them you can, and they you. This is the human norm says Diamond, the way we grew up in evolutionary time, the program that runs at the base of our awareness. Keep friendly with a few, exchange killings with a larger circle and fear those beyond.

War in this ritualized way doesn't work in our millions. The killing zone goes global as the weapons improve and the rings of mutuality melt away. The skin of civility is easily torn. Strongmen emerge from the shadows and let the violence ooze out.

What we evolved early on brought us dominance. Can we understand the program then graduate?

We'd become a new species. This will frighten many so we must care for them.

Map and territory

During the Second World War my father was in his twenties and the captain of a warship that crossed the Pacific to sail up the Yangtze. Training for the command in Key West he had a superior officer called Kellogg. This same Kellogg was to become an archetype for our family in later years. An archetype of dimness. Someone who confused the map with the territory.

Near the end of the training when my father and several other new captains were about to take command of their ships Kellogg met with them. He stood over a chart on his desk. The young captains had all trained in navigation and were an eager lot. Kellogg asked how long in their first deployment it would take to get to a certain place that interested him, a great many nautical miles away. The consensus of the captains was that it would take about five days. Kellogg exploded. He bent down to the chart, put thumb and forefinger over the distance then raised them. There were about two inches between thumb and forefinger. How can it take so long, Kellogg thundered, showing his fingers two inches apart, it's only this far!

Between friends

Saw a film that could have been scripted by Aesop. About tunnels under roads so creatures go safe. Florida panthers slink through, trucks roaring on the road above. Alligators stride as in the Pleistocene, ignoring the SUVs on top. Black bear families move fast, aware of the cars on the road but knowing they are safe below.

So much for the *mise-en-scène*.

There's a camera trap goes infrared for nightlife.

Fox shows up with eyes shining. Fox peers into tunnel then turns around and looks to camera with headlight eyes. Comes out of tunnel, looks to the right. Jumps up and down.

"Look what I've found, I told you so, this is totally great," is his manner. Then his friend comes into view, Badger. Fox goes into tunnel and Badger stays outside, skeptical, looking into the dark.

Fox turns around, eyes shining, "Come on let's go, this is going to be great."

Badger knows what Fox is thinking. Fox waits to make sure of Badger, who sighs and trundles in. Then together they set off through the tunnel for the night's adventure.

Badger's fat bum swings side to side as he hurries to keep up with Fox. Score for Fox, Badger, Aesop and tunnel builders.

The stars my companions

The stars have become my companions.

Living things always were. Now as I look out the window at night, the stars are my companions too. I offer greetings to all the enlightened beings living in the trillions of star systems out in the darkness before I fall asleep.

When I wake the Sun has taken the stars away. I lay over and listen to your heart.

Arriving

Always we're arriving

We may think we're trying to leave
when memory pulls

when we're pursued by anger
anxiety, abuse, abandonment

but night ends
day begins

We're always, always arriving

The Book of Memory

Empty air

Afterwards the air feels empty. In Evanston where you lived and have forever left, brother.

The cold hurts my feet walking along Lake Michigan's shore where fallen leaves bear the grace of frost before it melts in sun.

The empty air takes me past a coffee shop, its windows lined in a platoon of snake plants at attention then Trader Joe's to search for the last wine you had us serve up from your basement though you couldn't get down there yourself anymore or drink anything.

When we last spoke and hugged in the body I said in your ear that I'd always looked up to you and you said "I know babe but you were always the extraordinary one."

That radiance I looked up to is memory now in this empty air and distant and real and clear and hazy as tonight's full moon.

The store

The memory store has many products. I've been testing several.

One grows spontaneous from experience: I visit my parents' graves near the sea in California's winter. Emotion retrieves memories and new ones will grow.

One you assemble from printed instructions. The novelist writes the instructions, you assemble at home: turmoil after the death of Alexander, as Macedonian cavalry cut down Persian soldiers. The result's more intimate than meta worlds, since you made it. Memories follow.

Another you get from movies. Here's a film: a nurse takes care of an orphan during the Chinese Long March. You absorb it pre-packaged, but the impression is vivid. Memories follow.

In tranquil mind, each is visually precise. We can enter and navigate them from different angles. We can visit them and be inside.

Moving from one to the other what surprises me is how similar their textures, laid down through art or life. Woven of the same threads, as memories they feel equally real, equally part of my world.

Buffer

There's no end to memory, it feels like. We live and memories are kept. We don't run into a memory wall or find a full buffer. Next Tuesday won't lack memory space for what happens that day or the next.

Is memory potentially infinite but bounded by our lifespan, growing in richness and complexity, in reach and content, as we grow along our arrow of time.

Do some memories disappear from memory space like stars winking out and we don't notice since we can't see them anymore. Or do they exist quietly to be retrieved and reconstituted with the energy of intention, attention or medical inducement.

Are memories locked in our neural nets. Or are they uploaded to a cloud of knowing, a Cloud of Unknowing.

PLACES

We inhabit places in memory as in life. I stayed in an old hotel in Evanston for my brother's funeral. It was around Christmas, so the salon was decorated in a festive way.

The feeling of the place returns.

It's clear as the December light was then. A feeling of the place is built of memory. Like the buildings and rail lines, crosswalks and shops, spaces in the hotel made the physical place. That remembered place emerges or intrudes into waking life. Reality becomes dual.

Here now in this room with these feeling tones and also that room and those feeling tones. It's an offering of who you were then. That you and the present you, each as real as the other. That place coextensive with this one. If a memory is strong it can overwrite your experience of the place you are in now.

There opens an angle of sight and maybe insight. Visiting a place in memory is like visiting a person and talking with them.

Wearing away

Opening memories selects those we keep. Unopened ones drift away, evanescing like dreams. Ones we open and reopen build inner geography, places and times we can visit and revisit, landscapes of joy or suffering.

Long ago I read a Spanish poem. Writing as an old man, the poet recalled an important early love. He never forgot her and thought of her often. Now when he opened the memory, he was pretty sure her name was Maria, but the color of her eyes had evanesced.

Opening slightly edits memories, so we never visit the same memory twice. Synapses grow or decline as we choose memories to open. Touching memories edits brain. Some say we lose a little clarity each time we open a memory, as if they wear out like the face on a well-thumbed coin. As they wear, do they become less attached to the original facts, and become artefacts. Do they start to take the shape of the hour we reopen them and less of the hour they were laid down.

Visiting memories is like being a third party looking into a life laid open. Like being an artist looking at promising material, a scholar looking into a library of events and causes, a lover seeing the reasons for joy and regret. Like a ghost looking with interest into a living life, one's own living life.

Memory on pause

Memory draws a map of everyday life. The map unfolds as I open my eyes, see my room, my mate, meet with my colleagues at work, and stay in normal mind.

Go quiet though, go into awareness unbound by ego, then memory goes on pause. The personal drops away. Although impersonal, the experience is reassuring and welcoming, beyond ego's daily anxieties. You rest in a timeless moment.

But when *my* dog's bark calls me back, the coffee's taste is *my* experience, the instant anything is *mine,* then awareness is touched again by a thousand tendrils reaching up from memory's body and it's back to the daily round.

Joint memory

Marriages are made of memory. Melding builds new memories and we share intimacies all the way back to childhood. We tell those early memories again and again. New ones too. Telling and retelling, we live and relive them.

The first tellings lay down an architectural plan linking the pair. Retelling lays in the stones, builds a joint self. A time comes we don't know if it's my memory or hers, my memory or his. It's become a joined mind, joint being.

Joint memory is more important to our life than all the parthenons and palaces, all the pyramids and piazzas are to history. Joint memory is the virtual reality of the heart, the joined domain of self.

Joint memories endure till memory is wiped by illness or death, then survive in the other till their mind and body go. Joint memory is no less for being temporal and passing, a flower, a dragonfly, a galaxy.

Memory's end

What memory will play as I leave, leave for good, no returning.

What will memory finally touch.

Will it be an archive of grievance and disappointment.

Or will such afflictions drop away before I do, so memory offers my lover's skin, sunlight on sea, my mother's kindness, kneeling by a creek when we looked at fish and the little girl gave me a gap-toothed smile.

Letting the herd of grievances wander loose onto the plain of nonentity seems the goal to me today, the doorway to happy death, happy life.

Summer leaves

While I rest on its shore, the North Sea remains at work and reminds me of elements conditional to my cure: things are in motion at all scales so nothing is fixed or durable, everything we know recedes in the tides of time, consciousness is a brief light in the wide sea of space.

Memory returns another summer more than forty years ago. In the New York law firm Debevoise & Plimpton, my office is next to Eli Whitney Debevoise, tall elderly patrician founder of the firm, still in his office each day. I look into his eyes magnified by thick lenses. He asks am I there just for the summer.

When I agree, he looks through me and says, "Ah yes, they come and they go like leaves that turn colors and fall quickly to the ground."

I cannot help but like him.

Layers of consequence

I wake in Geneva one morning not long ago, and taxi to meet the head of a foundation. His office is on the top floor of a discreet glass building overlooking the lake.

After a few pleasantries, he tells me that my father taught him law many years ago. He says my father was loved by everyone, that he was a good man and a brilliant one with a sharp wit. He created an atmosphere of combined trepidation and excitement in his classroom that no one ever forgot. We all waited, he said, in case your father would call on us. We knew he would find us out if we hadn't prepared. Yet we all wanted to be called on.

I never expected to meet my father's memory alive and vivid in a high room overlooking Lake Geneva. Afterward my sense during meetings in city after city as I travel tired is that I too am aging. I wonder if I too may be remembered one day through a story shared in a chance meeting in a high building in a distant city.

Early waking in another new city with a Sunday ahead and a feeling of unease. How best use the day with time going and the world expressing its needs.

Inside it

Life living you. You living life. Pushing out to its edges with no space left. And then sometimes you feel the posture extended by your bones and know they hold you differently. You walk down the street and recall walking down the same street decades ago and sense how much brighter the colors were then and how much less detail lay in the shadows.

You see the thought you had was an echo of your mother's. You sense the smile you made was your father's smile, his gene expression and habit pattern, in turn reaching back up the tunnel of your ancestors. You sense the breadth of this seeing this feeling and it creates a space a perspective an envelope around the animal doing and you are not just living life then but know it at the same time.

Dog in the corner

That memory is a dog growling in the corner and I walk away from it. This memory is a sunny afternoon when anything was possible. I lay down into it when a virus pulled me to sleep this afternoon. Each memory's a chemical signature in my brain so recalling them is touching something physical like pulling out a museum tray and looking at the feathers of a bird of paradise.

It may be the specimen used to name the species yet it's physical and fragile and changes with each use. Like a memory does, rejigged each time, overwritten each time I call it up, changed each time it hurts or helps. Hanging out in the present this evening I leave my specimen cases of memory untouched for a while.

Swinging

Swinging up to sky higher and higher pausing near top never going over. Other kids say it's possible but you exercise your option to doubt. Later at home mom serves dinner. Inner ear repeats the day's play, still moving you up then down, an inner swinging private not over.

Crossing the Bay of Biscay overnight Plymouth to Santander, winds gale force 10, ship up then over wave tops then down into troughs repeating throughout the night.

The memory of my father visits, who captained his ship across the Pacific in a typhoon in WWII. I bend my right leg to bring right foot up to left knee, making a triangle as he taught me, so even a typhoon won't roll you out, and offer his memory my admiration.

Later that day, in Pau in the Restaurant Henri IV. At the table I sip local red. Inner ear returns the feeling of still moving up then over the waves then down into their troughs. Sitting at the table I'm still moving up then down, an inner swinging private not over.

Solaris

In Stanislav Lem's novel *Solaris,* and the film made of it, the planet Solaris captivates visitors. Structures rise from its seas into the air then fall back again always different always evanescent. The structures respond to the viewer to their feelings their intelligence their concerns yet the connection is never clear never direct and may be imaginary. The rising arcs grow vast and fall back. New patterns emerge always reshaping themselves through time through space. There is nothing you can finger nothing you can capture nothing that does what you expect nothing that resolves yet the planet's manifestations enter and change the visitor. A visitor becomes obsessed with the shifting structures, open to their play and wants more, looks for pattern looks for meaning. The more you attend to them the more hope deepens the hope always arising always disappointed that you will meet the intelligence behind the manifestations since you feel there is an intelligence big as the planet deeper and higher than your own.

As I play Bach solo violin works, I encounter a mysterious embedded intelligence behind them opening onto higher planes. The structures rise then fall away emotion building until it drops ever elusive no matter how many times I pick up my bow. Whenever I play and in between playing whenever these structures arise and fall in mind I visit Solaris.

Mirror of facts

no longer young
not yet old

no longer broke
not yet done

I hold up the mirror of facts
and see
simple wants make a happy life

The Book of Questions

Seamless

Assume the world is a simulation, run on a large system, perhaps coextensive with the Universe. Everything you see, everything you know, everything you feel, everything you taste, everything you think and everything you can ever taste, can ever think, can ever feel, can ever know, can ever see is part of this simulation. It's seamless.

What is the world simulating? It is simulating itself. Where does that leave you?

SAIL BACK IN GLORY

When Theseus sailed back in glory from his victories his ship became a monument to Athen's might. Time and shipworm ate away its planks to be replaced one by one. After all were renewed, philosophers asked was the ship the same ship that carried Theseus home.

The planks of my mind keep shifting. It's the vessel carries me through the years. Yet the neurons are replaced one by one and their connections reordered. Memories of earlier selves refashioned. Meanings shift in the mosaic of the whole. Others recognize my vessel as the same as it sails through life. From inside it morphs. Every day I wake surprised to be in a mind and a body. In this mind and this body. Present without explanation.

With an eye on Theseus's ship, Otto Neurath said we build knowledge like sailors mending their vessel at sea, plank by plank, troublesome below waterline. My planks are ripped out and replaced while moving through waves of real time. Rebuilt at need over the mystery of what lies damp in the hold and deeper below. One day this vessel will set out on the unknown sea like a Viking ship bearing a warrior's body burning. Will it be sailing back in glory?

On the side of things

Seas are restless though they seek no outcome. Storms threaten without intent to harm. Springtime comes gently though it's unstoppable.

What if we didn't project such dramas into things. What if we saw things straight. Perceived them. Received them. Didn't color them with emotion.

If the theater of our minds let *things* be the actors.

What if we took the side of things.

Would the world seem a friendly place. Or not. Would it shift back and forth.

Would Nature be our teacher.

Over tea

Over tea this morning I meet a scholar. He says our ignorance of the nature of things *"is so deep that it cannot depend on the experience of a single life but rather depends on the experiences of a multiplicity of lives."*

How can I make sense of this idea of rebirth, before my tea cools?

Something familiar arises: the span of evolution.

My ancestors back to annelid worms: we hate pain, love to eat and mate, and so our DNA gets reborn down the ages till now.

For millions of generations of beings, fleeing a predator was more important than insight. No time to sit staring into the pool while fanged predators prowl. So a scrim covers reality's depths.

You and I were born into a world where it's safe to sit and poke through the scrim.

But where is the need for '*my experience*' in all those prior generations?

'My' life is no other than experiencing the world through consciousness. Put the other way round, consciousness experiences the world through 'my' life.

Consciousness is widely distributed. It is no more mine than air is mine. Although air is not mine, my life intimately depends on it. Although consciousness is not mine, I do not exist apart from it.

What is this consciousness? It isn't nothing, since consciousness is clear and self-validating. It isn't something, since there's nothing fixed about it.

Not nothing, not something.

If I make consciousness my home, consciousness without beginning or end, then 'I' is just a motel room.

Next day's cup

My new friend has another thought for the day, about perception:

Mental consciousness, which is what we commonly refer to as "thought," or "our thinking mind," is unable to separate mental images from the actual bare perceptions, and is thus always *erroneous and distorted in that it confuses this mixture of mental image and perceptual consciousness for the object itself.*

We don't perceive the object itself. It's layered with associations and memories. Feelings are triggered. The object is a gift wrapped in layers of tissue.

Three of these gifts with their wrappings:

I walk into the kitchen. We are selling our house. As the summer sun lights the kitchen I'm aware a day will come soon when this kitchen is in the past. A wistfulness arises, a passing into history of the life we lived here with its rich and intricate story.

I pick up a roasting pan that was my mother's. Things that were hers have a resonance like religious relics did for medieval believers. It was touched by her and carries an aura that opens doors of memory to her caring, her unsparing work, her strength. All this takes no time, is simultaneous with picking up the pan, is picking up the pan.

My husband calls from India. A video call, I hear his adventures in Rajasthan, meeting members of the Bishnoi religion for his new book. Seeing his three dimensions brings in the time dimension. I've known him all these years, always changing and always the same, known and unknowable, the time dimension bringing depth of perspective as the moments move on.

No doubt, as the scholar says, all these perceptions are distorted and erroneous from one perspective.

From another they are just right. Their richness and subtlety is the poetry of perception and the meaning of everyday life. That's just how it works.

TRANSLATIONS

Experiencing what's far beyond our normal frame of cognition, some Zen and Hindu masters come back unsparing. Instead of stories of the ultimate, they tell us that anything that can be shared by thought is false, because thought itself separates. So, they say, there are no true words for what is beyond.

Others come back and translate. Mohammed hears his angel and writes verses from the desert. Luther's first thesis demands a life of repentance.

Translations find an audience. Coming back from the beyond with the news that non-thinking non-self is the reality, and being elusive about it, since you don't trust words, doesn't win as many friends.

Have the translations into the religions done enough though? Have the religions with all their millions of followers done more good than harm? That must be the test.

What's the needed translation now, one that would not harm but only help? Is it: Slow climate change, save Nature and love each other? Who would listen? Does that matter?

Fields of rapport

Were there no minds in the world, foxgloves would still balance light and water against gravity.

When I see a mountain, when I touch my lover's skin, feelings are part of the experience. No experience apart from these feelings. The feelings aren't extra. They're not in the mountain or the skin waiting to enter me. They're not placed onto the experience. I participate with the mountain, participate with the skin, each entering other.

Consciousness and object arise together in a field of rapport. The most natural thing in the world until we try to catch hold of it. It's like trying to catch hold of the taste of salt.

Does mathematics arise like feelings do and help make a world the way my feelings engage the mountain, the skin, the salt. For minds tuned to it, mathematics arises indivisibly from light, water, gravity, foxglove.

Other minds on other worlds have their own fields of rapport (could we recognize them as minds). Their own feelings (could we empathize) and mathematics (could we follow their equations). Do they find different feelings and different mathematics arising in their fields of rapport, remote from our abilities, it would be good to know.

Story of my death

Do I own my death. When I own something I can give it away. Not this.

Birth feels like I should own it in some way though. It is where the story starts.

Do I remember my birth. If I do not remember my birth how do I own it. I can claim it by telling a story.

Will I remember my death. If I will not remember my death how do I own it. There will be a death. There will be his death. In what way is it my death.

How can there be a my death. Perhaps as a story I tell myself. But that is fiction told before the day, a story about me as another.

How would I tell a story of my death as non-fiction, as owner of the experience. I'd have to do it after my death. Who would be the audience.

Some people

I love all living things (though there are some people I just can't like).

A hundred years ago, before life was unravelling, I might have been a biologist. Since the world is falling apart, I've spent more time on saving life than appreciating it, to my detriment.

Recently close to collapse myself, how to take care of life without feeling responsibility for all of it?

How to balance caring for all organisms with caring for this one, and his mate?

FURTHER

My concussion put mind and emotion under wet felt blankets.
Martin said "you were still there. You were still shining but your
light was hidden under heavy clouds." When Ronald Reagan's
dementia was getting worse Nancy said "Ron is still Ron but he
is going further and further away from us."

What was it shining out from under heavy clouds. What was it
going further and further away from Nancy.

Threshold

So this much is clear. Whether the Universe appears as a friendly place or not is our choice.

There's a threshold question for the next stage. How does enlightenment in one person help all beings? What is the tissue that connects them? Not metaphorically and not by way of wishful thinking but real as an octopus or car crash. If a person, call her Sofia, becomes deeply enlightened she might keep the fires of enlightenment burning so it does not go out in this dim world.

She might pour calm clarity on those she meets like a healing oil. And if she becomes a famous guru with a cable show she may reach a wider audience. But does this help all beings in a world close to the edge of collapse? Is deep enlightenment enough? How far do its ripples go out? How is it effective and for whom? How can Sofia make it so? That's the question.

Honest question

Out walking I meet a man, his brow furrowed by a question he carries.

"What is troubling you?" I ask and he looks up, relieved to be regarded.

"An honest question," he says, "and one that troubles me day and night. It is this: what would be the greater good for life in the galaxy–humans correcting their behavior and so succeeding in not extinguishing themselves–or humans crashing their own species so Nature heals on a personless world in time?"

After delivering his question he blinks, then walks on, brow furrowed, burdened once again.

Does happiness depend

Where does beauty go when it vanishes.
Why do people die when they are killed.
Why can't we touch thoughts.
Where does music come from.
Will the first artificial general intelligence love us back.
Why are we awake.
Where did all the antimatter go.

Does happiness depend on knowing.

The Book of Mind

Rules of the game

after Frank Ramsey

What would have happened had things been different.

If my team had won the game. If the natural world was thriving. If the bomb under the table had stopped the Führer. If I'd bought the winning ticket. If Wittgenstein were less troubled. If only she'd said yes. If Caesar had listened to the soothsayer. If Moctezuma had captured Cortes. If burning fossil fuel didn't cause global heating. If the Mongolian horsemen hadn't turned back. If Mozart had lived longer. If I hadn't been so lazy. If science had led to peace. If all the children had enough to eat. If her cancer hadn't been so painful at the end. If humanity had already gone through the bottleneck.

Before completing such thoughts note: statements about what would have happened if things had been different do not correspond to any reality.

At first a bright glazing

Fluid like a child running on a beach, that's how we start.

Then at first a bright glazing, that's how the self grows like ice on a river till free play freezes. Maturing is thawing.

When I have an unenlightened thought I am unenlightened, said old master Huineng.

An enlightened thought and I am enlightened, he said.

Freezing, flowing. Winter, spring. Moment by moment, it's like this.

Strange attractor

A word, what is it? A label slapped on something in the diorama of my mind? Mind's not a diorama though, nothing static. A word's more a strange attractor, a creature that lives in dynamical systems. A point where pattern emerges from chaos in mental space, a point pulling experience toward it. What happens around the point depends on how the language game begins.

Take bird. Bird starts with baby looking at duckling or robin or emu or junglefowl and talking to mom, first referee of words, to find a signifier for next time. That's bird.

The terms of bird shift and flow as baby grows and adds experience, of first bird seen from different directions in different lights, of female and male of first bird, of diverse patterns of color size shape sound behavior, of other beings who become bird.

These are pulled to the attractor, bird space in our mental field, so there evolves a dynamical understanding of bird never fixed but always moving. The same is true of girl or leader or love or winning, wisdom or word. Watch words self-organize in your mental space. You'll see.

Sparks

You don't need to invite them. They're there. They're quick. They flash. When you're brushing your teeth. When you're on the train. When you're open to noticing. They lie above. They're to the stream of consciousness what epigenetics is to genetics. The stream of consciousness carries us along. When it eddies it morphs into a train of thought and from the windows of the train you see your inscape pass by with all its elements viewed from the perspective of the train. These instead are flashes in the sky of the inscape. Flashes of memory and association that go by at the speed of synapses. No single long theme connects them. They're not a train not a stream. They reach across a disparate set of memories and associations. Each has a point of docking with another as they fractally emerge. They don't repeat the same patterns they don't wear a groove in consciousness. They catch a current moment then take it as a research project and project a light across the vast library of data inside you.

You can easily miss it because it happens so fast. If you latch onto one of the files as it flashes by then you turn on the spigot that leads to the stream that leads to the train. If you're attuned though you can fly above in the dome of the inscape and watch them light and go like sparks.

Other cities

In some dream cities I know the neighborhoods where it's unsafe to walk. Where my club is, with its quiet library and popular dining room. One city has elevators that move both vertically and horizontally.

Old master Aurobindo says your dreams take you to real places on other planes, real as your local reality. You can explore them. Remember them. Try recalling their color palette he says, and this will help you differentiate and recall. He visited worlds that were redder than ours and others that were yellower.

Whether Aurobindo is right about planes of reality, or my dreams are designed by a lonely artist in my cranium, I get a kick out of those sideways elevator rides, every time.

Complexity

In a book about AI, I read today: "Complexity means that the real-world decision problem—the problem of deciding what to do right now, at every instant in one's life—is so difficult that neither humans nor computers will ever come close to finding perfect solutions."

Then my husband and I went to a bodega where we perfectly solved the real-world decision problem of which bottle of wine to buy and then flawlessly took the real-world decision to watch the sunset over the sea and continued finding a series of perfect solutions instant by instant as we oriented ourselves facing west, drank the wine, and listened while the sea complemented the sky by throwing up real-world waves of perfect complexity.

The land of thought

Live in the land of thought, yet untouched by thought, said
    old master Fushan Yuan.

Live in the land of seeing and hearing, untouched by seeing
    and hearing.
See the sky fill and empty of clouds,
rain come and go,
politicians make promises then walk away,
flowers open and fall,
enemies and friends mature and pass,
species being discovered and going extinct,
the growth of love and turn of death,
the understanding and the refusal to understand,
the comfort and the cold,
and know them with equanimity.

It will take practice.

Think of it this way

Think of it this way. There is a cliff. You are facing it. Behind you is the accumulated weight of history. It is pushing you forward. The entire weight of history is pushing you forward. Before you lies the future. Where is your space to choose? How can you avoid being pushed off the cliff?

Think of it this way. It may be the entire weight of history. But there is no separating it from you. You are as much the cause of what comes next as any of it. As all of it. While there is no getting away from the cliff, your life and freedom are to be found in jumping.

Think of it this way. Every second of every day is a cliff. What are you jumping into? You are not separate from all the causes of history. Where does the question of free will come from anyway? The question is a knife separating you from everything else. A game to set you against the rest. Drop the knife. Stop playing the game.

Think of it this way. You were never separated from everything else. The future is set by you and everything else together. The future as it unfolds is music played in real time by this ensemble of you and everything together.

Think of it this way. When a rose grows it is part of the ensemble. The mind of God cannot see ahead and know the rose's color and shape in every detail. The rose co-creates its future. Which unfolds in its present among the harmonies and discords played by the whole ensemble.

Think of it this way. You can feel like you are about to be pushed off the cliff. Or you can hear the music and fly.

"...FOR THEN WE WOULD KNOW THE MIND OF GOD."

Stephen Hawking

The mind of God does not do theory. It works stuff out. It never strays from the present into hypotheses. It never moves from cause to generality. It never moves back from theory to practice. It just works stuff out.

We segment inspiration, theory, planning, doing. It does not. The physical manifestation is the calculation. Your body, your mind, that dog, the next tornado. Our future is a theory. For this mind there is no future. Only an evolving present. The past is our refuge. For this mind there is no past. Only the mobile present.

It has habits of thought. It usually does black holes like this, galaxies like this, origin of life on planets like this, orgasms like this. Tribal warfare like this, murder like this, enlightenment like this, cooperation like this, creative inspiration like this, extinction like this.

The events of the past echo as causes in the present. Call every local time in the Universe the present moment. Each being, each thing is in its own present. You included. Call each of them a thought. An original thought in this mind. You included. Each will become a cause for the next thought in the next present moment. You included.

All of them together always in the present without theory, just working it out without theory, only the present reality, this embodied reality, try that as the mind of God.

Now, tell me how tulips grow.

After humans

On the outskirts of discourse roam barbarians who celebrate our extinction. These nouveau barbarians congregate in two tribes.

The first watch us crashing the planet, and conclude we deserve to be wiped out.

They are wrong.

We got to the precipice by doing what all species do. Bacteria in a petri dish use all the food then die. We've been eating the planet, but only realized it yesterday, in the life of our species. We still have time to save civilization. If we don't it's a shame, not a punishment we deserve.

Who is there to punish us anyway? Hoping for our extinction is a failure of imagination. Wishing us away is lazy. Act. Civilization is worth evolving.

A second tribe want us to upload our minds and go transhuman. Or else create a universal general intelligence that surpasses us then keeps us as pets (or gets rid of us). Some of them want to commandeer every atom in the Universe, turn it into 'computronium', and make the Universe a computer modeled on our small dreams of consciousness.

They are wrong too.

The entire Universe is *already* Mind.

Every fish swimming, child dancing, orchid growing, star spinning, is performing more embodied calculations in real time through their ordinary life, movement, action, growth, than all atoms slaved together ever could. They interact ceaselessly toward a greater flourishing of Its evolving parts, most of them still unknown to us.

Don't wish it away. Take it as your teacher.

To those of you in these tribes. Join me.

Let's make things better for all beings everywhere.

WILDFIRE

it's fire
pouring through

an idea birthing
nostrils flare
air into lungs
heart races
it's physical
feeding it
till you're totally changed into fire

after
it's quiet
it's ashes
it's exhaustion
unable even to recall the feeling of what it was like

until the next fire

The Book of
Millions of Years

Songs to cross the threshold

after Gerard Grisey

Passerines flew up from Australia to radiate, speciate, fill the world and we call them songbirds. We know the songs of cicadas who grow slow underground and emerge in thirteen- or seventeen-year cycles, who with their stridulations outshout cement mixers. We know the trumpeting of elephants and the rumbling infrasound of their singing.

There are many more songs we do not know. Trees have songs. Butterflies have songs. Bluefin tuna flashing at the speed of cheetahs below the sea's curve have songs.

Let us discover them and save these songs. Let us imprint their songs on our being. Let their songs fill our hollow space of grief. Let us carry their songs and be shaped by their songs. Let us be shaped by them and see who we become.

For we too will go.

If we know their songs and sing them as we go then the butterflies the tuna the trees and whatever beings we leave behind will hear the songs we embody and gain the imprint of these songs as we cross the threshold. Then in their Earth home millions of years from now they will flourish again and become speciose again and numberless again and free to explore the sweet evolutionary shapes of Animalia, and find the newness they will need in the millions of years after we have gone.

Requiem for the Planet

Requiem for the Earth. Not yet. Requiem for Nature. Not yet. Requiem for Species. Yes, it's time for that.

Requiem for the Western Black Rhino, the Yangtze River Dolphin, the Ivory Billed Woodpecker, members of our Family. We need to acknowledge their passing, and the passing of many more, with ceremony.

What would a requiem for a species look like?

Let it be a time of celebration of the organism and its place in the web of life. Nothing quite like this species ever was before or will ever be again. It was a miracle thrown up by the Universe on the shore of Life.

Let us celebrate the life of the species by telling stories about where it came from, how it evolved. Celebrate its lifeways, its capacities, its special adaptations, where it fit into the web of life. Encounter its irreducible beauty. Enter into its radical uniqueness.

Then let us join together in a time of reflection. We take responsibility. We take responsibility that we, as members of the human Family, contributed to the extinction of the species.

This creature evolved for millions of years to be with us in our own time. It shared our world with us. Its path of millions of years is now closed.

We enter the truth that extinction is forever. There is no coming back. Nor is there any afterlife for the species to go on to.

This creature represented a lineage of sentient beings that is no more. We acknowledge that this is the time of extinctions, the Sixth Great Extinction.

We acknowledge our contribution to the death of this species and all its possible descendants through all of time. We accept that this is a kind of genocide. That the death of each individual species is a kind of genocide.

We vow to learn how to reduce extinction. We vow to reduce our contribution to extinctions. We vow to teach others, and do all we can to get countries and governments and companies to reduce the speed of extinctions, for the sake of all beings.

Now that we have told stories of the dead, reflected on our part in the death, and vowed to do better, let us celebrate with music. Let us join our voices to raise the roof with great music.

Let us sing songs to celebrate life, this species' life, and the life of all future life.

In this way, requiems for species become the source of our hope for all future generations.

THE LAST WORD

after Koun Yamada

Who has the last word. Will it be said. How will it be said. It will not be said by lips or tongue.

Whose word is it then. What says it will be said. Even if without lips or tongue.

What is the last word anyway. Where does the notion of a last word arise. Why assume it is a word at all.

Is it the last wave pushing against the shore on our planet's last day. Is it the fall of stars into black holes beckoning. Is it the endlessly slow and stretched out descent of the Universe into its final heat death over trillions of years. Is it that most intimate personal moment my consciousness like the consciousness of each one of us departs this sphere of reckoning.

Does the last word communicate anything. To whom would it communicate.

Does the last word have meaning.

Here we begin to see. The last word has no meaning.

Can it be perceived. It is beyond perception.

Is it something. It is nothing.

It is less than nothing.

Now what about the first word.

Becoming ocean

Walk beyond the human village. Let thoughts slow down and drop away. Let the adrenaline pulse of hectic messaging fall silent. Hear ocean. Depth of mind sound color.

Let your mind sink into ocean. At bottom we have a tacit understanding with ocean. What is it thinking, its body of billions of years, as it scrapes and caresses lands uninterrupted?

Perfect concentration ocean gives land, no distraction no tiring. Water fraying fabric of rock, its rhythms in tug with moon whose light silvers its surface. When a humpback sings a new song other whales pick up the tune and pass it on throughout world's waters.

What is lost as we acidify seas and bleach corals?

Permian, greatest of great dyings, saw almost all life extinguished. World ocean still rolled on caressing hide of continents. Life rebooted and has come down now to us.

Sleep

I trust sleep. The going away. The drop into void. Or a long breathing into darkness. Friendly or threatening experiences. The coming back. The return from encounters on the other side. Always coming back like coming to the surface with an aqualung. Will it be this way when I'm untethered. When there's no body to come back to. Will I surface from the dreams where I'm threatened like I do now. Pulled to the surface with hard heartbeat and heavy breathing as I am now.

Or when there is no substrate in the world will I wander life to life with no central story no watcher in the tower of life's landscape. Is death a dream we don't return from. Or is death a dreamless sleep.

You are often in my sleep. Wake and you are always there. Were I to wake and you were there no longer would I want to wake again.

Flourishing and
Extinction

It's not an easy story: birth and death. But why make it a story. It's just birth and death. Birth is birth. Death is death. Flourishing is in between. If there is flourishing. So why make a story of birth and death. Because we make everything a story. My birth and my death. In what way is it mine.

Does my death represent all death. Does it let me understand the death of others. Is my death representative of the death of classes of beings, of species. Species are dying every day. In what way is my death like the death of a species. Or is a species dying more to be mourned, more to be missed, as a deeper rent in the flourishing. Because there was flourishing.

Every kid is a story monger. We are made of stories. If we make stories of everything we do, do we make stories after death. In death do we move from story to story inside them experiencing them, being different characters having the experiences. Freed of a human body do we move from plane to plane of existence. Is it like moving from one dream straight into another dream. With this difference, that there's no body, nobody, to wake up into. Death would then be not a dreamless sleep but an endless dream.

Will there be rhinos after death. I would miss rhinos. Not all rhino species have been extinguished. Made extinct. Extincted. So will there be rhinos. Will I be capable of missing rhinos after I die. Will I be capable of missing. Will I be capable. Will I be I. Will I be. Will I.

Among trillions of galaxies, we sit inside self-reflective conscious-ness. We can turn the lamp of consciousness back upon ourselves. Alone together in such minds far as we know. Just as all of us die, all species go extinct. Will we go extinct or break the rule when some descendant evolves into a new lineage. Will they live on till heat death collects the stars. Or will our species commit suicide by chewing life down to the bone.

If there is no one left to sing sea shanties will the oceans be lonely.

Constant Creation

Today I visited the engines of Creation, birthing place for stars that join in galaxies. Stellar firmament extended filmy in all directions where space, light years across, blazes orange red beyond the realm of senses to gather or contain yet open to perception.

I admired the scope and power, bathed in the radiance, swam in timeless time. Then I was given a teaching by the Mind constant in creation, which said:

There is no hatred in Creation.

Creation does not make hatred.

Hatred is made by man.

A dark spot appeared in the radiance, to show what hatred would look like in the womb of creation. The spot was wiped out, the creative process returning to its nature, its demonstration done. The creative force, I then perceived, is never marred by darkness or separation, which call hatred into being.

Though not separate from this Mind and its firmament I rested distinct from it, small and on the side. I offered gratitude, wiped my tears, and was away, graced and changed.

Iris

iris of my eye
featureless and dark
information falls in
light falls in
and doesn't come out

the black hole
at the center of our galaxy
was imaged this week
its dark iris
surrounded by a cornea
of glowing gas

what is our black hole
seeing

The Book of
Compassion Arising

Rare visa

I've never been a tourist anywhere I like as much. My visa was hard to get. It's not tightly time bound. I can stay eighty-five years, with possible extensions. Never before have I visited a planet like it. The human form is comely. The human lifecycle sexy. The human consciousness one I like being in. Though bounded by the needs of this ape species it opens to the full suite of Mind.

On this planet there is uncountable suffering to learn from. Uncountable love to give. The dynamics of those who live for power not wisdom play out everywhere. The demagogues who display like apes beating chests by cutting down rainforest. By drilling for oil where it kills whales wiser than them. By promoting development where it brings extinction to species senior to theirs.

But there is also this: I watched a poor young black male in the land of Brexit who cared so much he took off his coat in the cold for an old white drunk and stayed with him until the ambulance came and saved the old man. I had not predicted the like. I had not seen it before. It did not fit into the patterns repeated in their news. There's so much to learn in this school of Earth while I've got the rare visa to be here.

America in the streets, June 2020

I see the streets of my broken homeland full of rage at the murder of George Floyd.

Then go quiet, asking where our life comes from, what impulse drives its deepest layers.

Physics offers four fundamental forces: gravity, the weak force, the electromagnetic, and strong force. I wonder if there's a fifth fundamental force, deeper than all the others, a force our organism senses and which bubbles up into our poor taxonomy to get called love.

Marking love as the organizing principle of the Universe, the ground of our essential unfolding. Knowing this would let us see that turning away from love is like turning away from gravity. You can't do it without falling.

Cataract on the heart

Can I get out the door without taking prejudice along. Sticking to my eyes every day all these years. Seeped in with TV when I was young. Not me but clings like oily fingernail dirt hard to get out. I know better but it lives inside and rises every day. Attention should scrape it clean like a sandstorm would. It puts up filters though against what could otherwise pour in to sculpt me better.

There's so little time to learn and so much territory to open. Prejudice knows my inner contours with instant precision. It keeps out facts that could baffle and change me.

Prejudice is a cataract on the heart that keeps me from fronting facts and living real. Time to break the seals. Smash the filters. Pick out the shards for as long, and it is long, as long as it takes to see clear.

Old master Dogen said that enlightenment is like meeting someone and not thinking about what they look like. That's what I want.

Closer every day

Some days the sadness is so deep I can't speak, so walk for hours hoping to hear a bird, a single one.

Sadness I wear like clothes and drink like wine. It penetrates. Let the sadness grow. Let it sink down till there is no motion. An absolute zero of the mind unmoving.

Not wishing it different. Steeping in it, you come to know it intimately. And learn it is no other than bliss and repose. This sadness the heaviness of bliss. This inability to speak the sign of repose.

Gratitude comes then.

Let it flow the gratitude. Let it flow into thanksgiving for the senses. Let it flow into blessings for the mind and all of being. Let the blessings flow.

What was was good. What is is now. What will come will be. It will not be what it could have been had we learned to love the living world as ourselves. Not as much as ourselves but *as* ourselves. It will not be that. No not now. That's now beyond grasp. Bind the wounds of the present.

Something will come. It does not need to be perfect to be wonderful. Let it be the most bountiful living world we can together make. Let it come let it come let it flow into the bliss and repose always there and always unbroken.

Going back to Mosul

On the radio in the middle of the night Martin heard a young man speak. Living in Iraq the young man dreamed of becoming a plastic surgeon to help a disfigured man in his village. Then at 17 he was playing basketball when a man of middle age drove a truck up to the boys playing ball, smiled at them, and blew himself and his truck up, a suicide bomber. The boy flew into the air, landed on his face and was blinded. He was left for dead among the bodies of the other boys. When his father came to claim the body, it started speaking. The boy was airlifted by Americans, kept alive.

Later, when his brother saw him he did not recognize the boy due to his destroyed face. *Médecins Sans Frontières* took the boy and operated on him thirty-five times but said he would never see again. The boy went to America and learned how to tutor other blind people. He then went back to Mosul to devote his life to teaching blind people there. He now thanks God that he is blind. He never looks back. To look back is to get stuck in history, he says. Only by asking how can I help today with what I have today, can a man live the right way. He says he would not choose sight over blindness because he has found his way and his work.

Sometimes a person distills wisdom from suffering by entering the mystery, performing the miracle, embracing the real with no distractions.

Not owning

The other night a philanthropist friend said that his talent was making money but he didn't own the money. He was only the custodian, and must do good with it. He went on to say we don't own the Earth but are only its custodians and must do good toward it. He said that this is our work and that it is spiritual work.

While I listened to him I realized I don't own my mind and talents. My abilities are not my own. I'm just their custodian to do good for the Earth and all who live on her.

From an angel's journal

When it comes to flying I'm familiar. I sometimes fly about a foot above the ground exhilarated like a wolf. Sometimes fast and clear like a raptor. In the world I come from flying is my special joy and an expression of who I am.

It's when I come back to the world of people there's a problem. Their mental knots and emotional binds throw up nets that arrest me and catch me in flight. Conscious and unconscious in design their traps are their shadows, the other side of who they could be.

Because I care for them I allow myself to be caught and spend most of my time untying the knots in their nets. Trapped to help them. Breathing harder, not flying, not seeing the Sun. Each of their knots untied is a measure of my success, of what I live for.

They were created to fly but refuse. They prefer to sit in the mud and throw up traps so fast it's a question whether I can untie the knots quickly enough. I'll keep on because while I do it gives teeth to hope.

Where does compassion come from

Where does compassion come from? How does it fit into our world?

Our World is what we perceive, a subset of the Universe, the subset our senses and mind allow. Our World is made of things. Things exist independently of us: stars, hamburgers, the children next door. The sum of things is the basis of our reality.

We receive and perceive this reality. To it we add feelings and emotions. These give birth to attachments. Attachments are the source of suffering.

Now move to Mind, or the Source, or the Ground of Being. It creates the Universe continuously. It suffers no feelings or emotions, generates no attachments, experiences no suffering. To the degree we enter Mind we loosen attachments. To the degree we loosen attachments we reduce our suffering.

Feelings and emotions still arise but don't so readily bind us. We gain space to see other people's attachments, see how their attachments bring them suffering, how their suffering brings suffering to others.

To the degree we see these dynamics compassion can arise. Compassion arises delicately and intermittently at first. Compassion grows with Mind time. Compassion is not a feeling or an emotion. We do not add it to the reality of things.

Compassion is the creative force of Mind expressed within the human domain.

I'm trying to get there. Join me.

Into this world each day

I am father and mother to hope. Hope is the child I bring into this world each day, show her ways to grow, point out ways he can mature.

As the face in the mirror changes year by year, I've learned we need to make time. We need to concentrate. We need to pay attention. We need to love the world, all its people, all its living beings, every one of them, all of them together.

Not just fearing for them, not just mourning their passing, not just fighting to protect them, not just working to heal them, but loving them without judgment as if they were our hope, our children, as if they were spring petals on dark ground.

Progress

Progress through the calendar is progress of a kind. Progress through water is progress of a kind. Kindness is progress too.

Kindness knows no barriers as it progresses through obstacles. Barriers are raised and barriers are fortified. Kindness moves around them and over them. Kindness finds chinks in barriers like water does.

Water is stable yet rises in waves. Kindness is stable yet rises against injustice.

Wherever it emerges kindness is progress.

Present

Being in the present is being in the Presence. Being in the present is being the Presence.

When we are given a human body, we are given a tool of the Universe, said old master Dogen.

Being in the present makes that tool available.

By being in the present we make our body a present to the Universe.

Cup

It takes practice
filling the cup I'm used to draining.

Drops of patience
atoms of insight, bits of resilience.

When it's half full, I'll declare victory.

The Book of the
Warming Earth

Augury

In Hackney Marshes I practice augury.

If gods exist they communicate, and birds are messengers, since they're closer to heaven than we, said the ancients. Augury stretches back before Rome to Egypt and Chaldea. An augur sees signs in birds' flight patterns, their numbers, and which species show up. An eagle's more auspicious than a sparrow.

Romulus and Remus argued over putting Rome on the Palatine or Aventine Hill. Sitting down, they settled it with augury. Each took half the sky. Remus counted six vultures. Romulus won with twelve and donated his name to the city.

It's the hottest day in English history, today. I do an augury on our warming world.

Take half the sky. Wait. No birds. Nothing to interpret.

Empty sky didn't happen when ancients did auguries. Empty sky doesn't feel auspicious.

Sustaining itself

A forest sustains itself. Controls who lives and grows there. Creates the local climate. It may live ten thousand years while its members flicker in and out. It needs a certain mass and moisture. Amazon greatest of shamans has anciently maintained itself and breathes for the world while nourishing the greatest variety of living beings.

When enough is lost though, maybe a quarter, its power goes with all it conjures. Three great droughts already in this short century suggest the forest nears a tipping point. The system is oscillating and may come down on the side of loss.

Pudding bowl

He needs me to understand about pudding bowls, the physicist I meet. A hollowness of enormity in the bedrock darkness. Under western Antarctic's ice sheet. Shaped like a pudding bowl and filled with ice to overflowing.

The pudding bowl lies below sea level, its lip not far from the sea. Sealed by ice for now. The sea is warming and will melt the ice. Seawater will slip over the bowl's lip then nothing will slow inrushing seas. The ice will float and global seas rise six meters.

Not for hundreds of years, I say. The seal could melt soon, he says, and water rush in to fill the bowl within a decade after. Talk of pudding usually cheers me.

Concerned now

They're lit at night so I can see thirty supertankers from my window on the North Sea. They're tethered riding full. The pandemic pushed fuel prices down and they're waiting to sell high. The world is moving away from fossil fuel people say. But today *Nature* asserts a different view and says just ten percent of electric utilities are on the path away from fossil.

I've been on a retreat this August looking out to sea. Tomorrow back to work. We'll sue oil companies and power plants, banks that finance them. We'll get laws and shareholder resolutions passed. Stick in the lever and pull. Result of my being here now, concerned now.

Apricot

Today an aching sadness entered, from studies I absorb while home with a virus, studies about cascades of disruption that global heating brings.

Usually it's a cerebral walk, this excursion into future pain. Maybe it was the illness today slowed the pace and opened the heart to the coming changes for all lives. In this dynamically interactive space of sadness this deep connected unfocused sadness this feeling that is rare I happened to eat a dried apricot and its bowl of taste spilled over.

When will the space open up for an apricot to taste so sweet again.

Nowhere to build an ark

My skiff rides shining Alaskan seas. They fizz around me in millions, the krill. Fish leap excited and a whale's over there. Pink crustaceans, down into darkness during day, up to feed at night. Lucky ones live ten years. Sea ice algae feed them but the ice is melting, so krill are three quarters down, fewer with every melting berg. Penguins and seals, fish and whales follow them in plummet. The charismatic depend upon the small.

Megafires were new to California these recent years. They arrived uninvited. Expect more. Firefighters from Australia fly in to help when not occupied with the same down under. Look at Canada and the USA. Ten million acres scorched this year. Sweden burned too. Sweden. Followed by Russia, Alaska, the Amazon. "Huge wildfires defy explanation," headlines *Nature*.

Seems to me we might have entered the Pyrocene, the Age of Fires.

I walked into sadness in Oxford one day. My vision was written over. I saw what will come. The quads were not green but filled with sand; sand poured up the steps by wind. I tasted desert dust sharp and bitter. Oxford become Morocco. Wide awake vision on a weekday tells me what is coming more than all the science. Coming soon. I know. I saw.

Piece of paper

Yesterday my physicist friend and I got drunk. Our minds reeling
we agreed

the global system is so close to tipping points it will edge over.

Today I'm feeling how quickly life passes, how fast civilizations go.

It's like tearing a piece of paper.

Everyone writing

Everyone writing hopes they will be remembered in a hundred years like Joyce, a couple hundred like Austen, a couple thousand like Sappho. None will.

Unless global heating is throttled back, the stories we tell will be forgotten as if we'd never lived. The theories we launch, companies we found, discoveries we make, buildings we build, hopes we realize, rainforests we save, artificial intelligences we create, Indigenous peoples we empower, democracies we nurture, lives we save, children whose minds we open, works of art we make and conserve, all of these, unless global heating is throttled back hard and fast will be ephemeral as verses traced on the surfaces of streams by mayflies.

Elective indifference

Flying London to LA I read climate science for eleven hours. I know the findings before I start but marathon reading raises my feelings up in line with facts and puts me on edge.

Off the plane, walking the sunshine, its warmth doesn't penetrate. We are stumbling.

Civilization can go.

The end of the human project bothers me more than my own death. My death is inevitable; the death of civilization is not. If it happens it will be elected by our indifference.

LAST THREE WEEKS

Three solid weeks before I got here California had big rain: thirty
trillion gallons,

while its worst drought in twelve hundred years ran on in the
background.

Looking around you wouldn't know anything had changed or
anything was wrong. Plantings are manicured, cars are hot, men
are buffed and tanned, women are waxed and polished.

This way of living is so creamy and appealing it drives me crazy
it's leading to the end of civilization.

Biggest risk

At a climate conference, a government official came to me and said, "I have something urgent to tell you. But I must say it quietly."

Quietly, he said, "Politicians who deny climate change—like many Republicans in the US—and leaders who do nothing—like the UK prime minister—are security risks. Let me underline that: *security risks.* These people will collapse civilization in a few decades through stupidity and inaction. Forget terrorism. These people are cementing the foundations of a global genocide. Why do I say genocide rather than tragedy? Because they could prevent it. They occupy the positions of responsibility and are letting it happen. It is on their hands."

I listened, and he added, "I have to say this quietly, given my position. I can't say out loud that our leaders are our biggest security risk. Now it's up to you. Go out and amplify this message. We have to replace them with people who take climate seriously. It's not too late. But it's almost too late."

Upon reflection, I can only agree.

Now, how to amplify his message.

Midnight

Midnight in San Francisco airport. Here for a climate conference. Time distorts and I look inward. Who am I tonight. What answers come. Echoes of intention across the inner landscape: I want to stop civilization's collapse.

It's been building, this intention.

People have moved me all day with their ordinary passions. Three young men in the Chinese restaurant believing in their future. Tired travelers tonight chatting on their cell phones. Children whining nearby.

Living lives, unseeing of the precipice ahead. Not knowing the ordinary is no longer ordinary. I feel for them. See them from a distance. Sad, sober, more than ever dedicated to their future.

Burning

The countryside is burning.

                    Making the right decision

The taiga is burning.

                    is far from guaranteed

The mountains are burning.

                    since evolution gave our brains

The rainforest is burning.

                    many inbuilt biases, so

The world is burning.

                    our impulse is to behave in ways

The world is burning in many

places all at the same time.

                    that defy logic and good sense.

The Book of Anxiety

ALREADY HARD TO FOCUS

Two days ago Notre Dame Cathedral burned. It got more attention than the suffering of the living world. Left to choose I'd pick coral reefs over Notre Dame.

Our own mental health depends intimately on a healthy world. Soon there will be no respite as the world heats more and systems fail. We find it difficult to focus on what is meaningful. We've found it so even when we lived in a flourishing healthy world.

How much more difficult when we find there is no safe place to stand. People become agitated in the heat and violence soars. What about when this becomes general. We will have no place of greater safety to retreat to. Who will be able to focus on what is meaningful then. Who will stay sane. Who will help others remember it is possible to be sane. Or what sanity looks like.

Environmental problems are mental problems.

Environmental problems are mental problems

Environmental problems are mental problems.

This is true both as cause and as effect. As cause, environmental crises are born of our mental problems. As effect, we get mental problems due to environmental crises.

Environmental problems are caused by our mental problems. It is our thought forms being out of alignment with reality (here read natural systems, the real world, the world beyond our heads) that has gotten us into the crises.

If we were thinking straight there would be no environmental problems. If we were thinking straight we would not have caused them. If we had built our civilization to interact harmlessly with the natural world, we would be thriving. So would the world beyond the human village. But our shared mental realm has drifted deeply out of touch with reality.

To be deeply out of touch with reality is to have mental health issues. That's the definition of mental problems. If someone walks down the street thinking he's Napoleon or Jesus, we have no problem saying he has mental health issues.

Now imagine someone walking down the street thinking that he and the natural world are separate, that he is meant to dominate the natural world rather than harmonize with it. Isn't he as crazy as someone who thinks he's Napoleon?

Someone denying climate change is like this. The same for a Brazilian president hell bent on cutting and burning the Amazon. Or a company president pumping ever more plastics into the world. And so on down the scale of not meshing with the inter-dependent reality of the living world.

Environmental problems also bring us mental problems. Here anxiety.

We must remember that as heat goes up, violence soars. This is well understood. As the situation becomes worse, the ability to make rational decisions will deteriorate and there will be a tendency for more primitive and less useful thought forms to emerge, compete and dominate. Staying sane enough to make wise decisions, rare among humans in the best of times, will become yet harder.

While addressing the physical environmental problems, how can we also address our mental health?

Mind cleaning

Maladaptive thought forms have led to the environmental crises we find ourselves in, with all their human sequelae.

We need to change our minds.

Getting rid of maladaptive thought forms is like waking from a dream.

When you wake from the dream of dominance and separation, you want to take care of the natural world and the people who are part of it. You want to take care of everyone. Even the bad actors.

Your anger directed at them drains you. What sustains you is turning the anger and anguish into positive action. Any positive action.

When the flood follows you, when the fire chases you, there are no longer enemies.

Now what about the mental problems that the environmental crises will bring, and are already bringing.

Dealing with the mental and emotional confusion that global heating will bring is also like waking from a dream.

The difference is that—unless we engage in radical change—we will wake up to find that we are in a nightmare. And that nightmare will be the real world.

If this is where we wind up, we will all have anxiety and it will be part of every day. We will need to tend our minds, soften our hearts, accept our anxiety and work with it. Then we will need to take care of each other, take care of everyone living together in the world we made.

Having the motivation to take care of everyone, finding meaning in taking care of them, finding joy in what remains of the natural world, saving what remains of the natural world. That will be our job.

We will be able to do this because a nightmare is not the end of our story. A nightmare is something we live through.

Anxiety, today's exit strategy

Hoping the surface doesn't break. Will it hold.

My movement is hesitant and calculated. Hoping the ice reaches the bottom to keep the kelp and seaweed still. Hoping it freezes leviathan and kraken. Their dark hungers reach out to me.

Hip aches. Evidence that I'm awake now, no longer dreaming. No light comes through the window. Darkness is profound. Silence too. Heart races.

Anxiety's spilled over into my waking world from dreams. A storm blows through my inner landscape. Drips adrenaline into my bloodstream. Time to calm the animal.

I tell myself: everything is all right, everything is okay.

Gently as I would to a child, a horse, a dog. I say it over and over until it becomes a mantra, everything is all right, everything is okay. Over time with patience I feel the heart rate go lower and the breathing get shallow. Everything becomes all right. Everything becomes okay. Then I'm gone.

5:30 A.M.

I wake at 5:30, heart racing, with the thought I've not done enough to stop climate change. There's truth in the thought. At a certain level of repetition, it's a helpful prompt to do more. But when it slides down from goal and goad into anxious self-criticism, perseverating, relentless and unanswerable, it becomes acid dissolving my life.

Once upon a time in Boston I met a psychic. She said, let me tell you a story about a past life you had. You were on a planet in a distant solar system. Its civilization was under threat from the ecological damage they were wreaking on the planet. You dedicated your life to stopping the destruction, to saving the people, saving the civilization. You spent your whole life at this task. But it was too far gone. You failed. The civilization collapsed and you saw it collapse. It was personally devastating for you. So you were born here now on Earth with the experience of this tragedy hard wired into you, so you could try again, could try to save the Earth. That's why you do what you do, and why this challenge will never let you go.

My need to help needs help. I'll do a better job if I can sleep.

Kids are hurting from climate anxiety

Young people around the world are hurting. Climate anxiety is widespread, endemic, deep and increasing. It deprives young people of a sense of agency, as they perceive a dying world they cannot save. The American Psychiatric Association defines eco-anxiety as "chronic fear of environmental doom".

Today scientists from around the world said it's getting near impossible to hold global heating to 1.5C, without action far beyond what any government is doing, or even planning to do.

The dream of 1.5C, enshrined in the Paris Agreement, is slipping, and the next notch is 2C. Sounds innocuous till you realize that compared to 1.5C, the fall in crop yields doubles at 2C; three times as many people will be exposed to deadly heatwaves at 2C; coral reefs move from the emergency room to the morgue. So at 2C say goodbye to coral reefs, the millions of creatures they nurture, and people they feed. Beyond 2C, agonies multiply.

Tens of thousands of school kids in France are already being medicated for mental health issues caused in part by climate change, said a recent news report. Three quarters of kids in the UK age 16-24 say climate change negatively affects their mental health.

It's the same around the world. The kids are paying attention. Their anxiety is a rational response. This makes climate anxiety different from traditional anxiety disorders.

Those who suffer from traditional anxiety disorders can be told their anxiety isn't based on facts. This helps.

It's different with climate anxiety. *It arises from the facts*. The fact is that civilization will collapse unless radical action is taken *now,* action no government is even thinking about seriously. The more clearly you see this, the more your anxieties arise. To treat the source of the anxiety we need to treat the world as our patient and reduce global heating, the planet's fever.

Global heating isn't going away.

So we need to accept that people with open eyes will have climate anxiety and in many it will be severe. We need to treat climate anxiety as a chronic illness rationally arising.

It's Nature too

It's not just climate, it's Nature too. Understanding the scale of damage is hard when it's presented as the numbers of species lost or explained as complex events in faraway forests.

So a new study is eye opening. Scientists looked at the weight of animals. It's like getting on the scale. We all dread that weighing up, but know it's important.

So how is the natural world weighing up?

All wild animals on the surface of the planet weigh in at twenty-two million tons.

On the other side of the ring, humans weigh in at three hundred and ninety million tons.

When you add our pigs, cows, chickens, and so on, we weigh in at a *billion* tons. All wild animals weigh in at just *two percent* of our combined avoirdupois.

No wonder who is winning in the ring.

Let's talk pets. Dogs tip the scales at the same weight as all the wild animals left roaming our lonely world today. Cats weigh as much as all the elephants left in Africa, and elephants don't eat meat.

How's your sense of perspective?

Anxiety arising from the body

Anxiety arises from the mind as a rational response to climate change. Anxiety also arises from the body.

To set up ClientEarth, I moved to London. I wanted to clean up the air. I knew living in London's dirty air would likely shorten my life. Walking around Mayfair to raise money against global heating left my lungs burning. The hurt in my lungs gave rise to anxiety in the body.

Stay with this body anxiety, and consider losing the natural world.

We are wiping it out faster than most of us realize. Knowing the facts raises anxiety. Like climate anxiety, this is a rational response. But it's more than just reason that's involved. Anxiety at the loss of Nature is body anxiety too.

My body is Nature and Nature is my body. My body is no other than Nature and Nature is no other than my body.

Harm to Nature is harm to my body. When any species of beetle goes extinct in the Amazon, I am diminished.

How to work with such anxiety?

Let your anxiety out of the closet. It's real. It means you are aware and paying attention. Let your anxiety move you to action. At first anxiety takes away our power and strangles our action. But when you liberate the energy of anxiety, and the energy of anger behind it, you are in charge of a powerful force. Channel this energy into positive action. Doing something positive gives you agency. You no longer feel powerless.

My way in recent decades has been to set up ClientEarth, to use the power of law for the planet. We can all find myriad ways to do something positive for the climate, for Nature. Study the problems and find the ways.

When you vote, demand your politicians act. Demand they become the first in the world to make radical change for the climate. If you run a company make it carbon neutral fast. If you have a pension watch where your money goes and insist it doesn't add to the burning.

If you are young, know that depression and cynicism about solving the problem are among our biggest enemies. You can act. Every .1 degree of climate change averted is an immense victory, on the scale of winning a world war. So bug your parents. Act at school, act at university, join other young people. There is an immense and growing worldwide movement led by young people.

Since climate change affects everything, there is a string of the solution for everyone to pull. Find your string and pull.

Also, there's something very important to remember that helps to counteract anxiety, mitigate despair and puncture cynicism. Remember to appreciate. To appreciate life, to appreciate the life of all life. Every weed, every bird, every insect, anything with a touch of wildness gives us hope, and reminds us of freedom.

One of our main jobs as people is to appreciate Nature.

Since Nature is our body, to appreciate Nature in its smallest and seemingly insignificant manifestations is to appreciate our own life. To take care of it is to take care of ourselves.

Flying to Johannesburg

In the air, halfway across Africa, that's when the storms begin, storms in my inner landscape, in my nervous system. It starts with the feeling of not enough breath, that I'm not getting enough air, so I get anxious, though I know that I do have enough, that my alveoli are functioning smoothly.

Reason doesn't calm it and the anxiety does its own rounds, self-reinforcing, escalating, so I watch while it happens.

Then the electric storm kicks up in my nervous system. Quickly it builds till it feels like I'm attached to a powerful battery. My system from head to tail lights up and I can feel the hot nerves clearly, see them in my mind. (When I later check anatomical drawings of the nervous system, I will find my feelings and images were exact.)

The discharges happen not once, not ten times, not a hundred times but once a second. Powerful electric shocks pulse and flash around once a second again and again, and this goes on for half an hour so say eighteen hundred times.

I talk to all the buddhas and enlightened beings in the Universe and ask for help. They are there with me but it doesn't stop, so I surrender and let myself be taken. Barriers get broken down, and in the days after I am fragile.

January London

I return to London on an overnight flight from Joburg, hoping the anxiety doesn't repeat. I don't want anxiety today. I don't want ecstasy today. I broke through to ecstasy from anxiety on the flight down, but it's not something I want on every plane flight. Ecstasy takes time to recover from.

The trigger was stress and so I've calmed the nerves.

For nine weeks in South Africa I've worked on unapologetic rest. No work, no decisions, nine weeks in nature, breathing exercises from the Mayo clinic.

Seated on the plane on the way back I talk to my ancestors, ask for their help, go into meditation. Calm descends and it's clear the long night flight will be untroubled.

Once back in London, a small but annoying interaction with my office brings back a cascade of stress. As if stored up, it flows out, heart rate over a hundred all night, lack of sleep. It's like being sick. Is being sick.

Next day it's resolved. Heart rate down, stress down, wellbeing back.

It's useful, this episode. To see how overwound the donkey was, how easily triggered he still is, how much pasture he needs.

My twin sisters

I've been ruled by my twin sisters, Duty and Anxiety. Duty made me work to save civilization and nature. Anxiety counseled I was never doing enough, never working hard enough.

Things hotted up a few years ago when Anxiety reached into my dreams and choked me awake for a panic attack.

I woke gasping, in the classic manner. You think you can't breathe and are going to die. Years of meditation meant I had a dual perspective. Feeling I was going to die from lack of breath, while at the same time watching myself, knowing I was going through a panic attack and would survive.

The part of the brain Anxiety squeezed into panic is immune to reason, far from language, old as lizards, and so the attack ran its course an hour or more, me watching and tending myself as if I were a needy friend.

After her first success, Anxiety toned down her interventions for some years. Recently though she's found a new gambit. Not panic but anxiety attacks came. Intense, but not as if you are about to die.

Anxiety started this new round of attacks after I stepped down as CEO of ClientEarth and went on sabbatical. The timing surprised me since there was no more daily stress to enter life. But bottled stress, it seemed, could be let out now, so stress distilled over years spilled out of the bottle and overflowed as anxiety attacks. Anxiety was taking the opportunity to let her genie out of my bottle.

Going deeper means learning where the attacks come from and how to take care of them.

The attacks circle around breath, am I getting enough oxygen, am I breathing well enough. The anxiety finds a tether in my asthma, my pneumonia, lungs being my weak point, my mother and grandmother dying of lung cancer, my susceptibility to burning in the lungs from air pollution. Breath is a good place for Anxiety to fix her tether. She adds electric storms in my nervous system for good measure.

This morning, after a night free of anxiety, the question emerged hard—since you are no longer running ClientEarth, what justification do you have for living?

It was my twin sisters confronting me at 6 am. They showed me unhappy hours and days stretching ahead into years. Without Duty and Anxiety to mesmerize and direct me, my mind and heart would become featureless empty geography.

Something was needed to placate the sisters. I offered three gifts: working on climate change, writing, going deeper. They were happy with these, since they offer innumerable opportunities for Duty and Anxiety to slip back in.

I wasn't happy though. I want to ease my twin sisters into retirement.

In a moment of radical self-preservation, I chose a new goal: to appreciate my life.

It will take practice. It's peeling back the layers laid down by Anxiety. It's discovering the way Anxiety has permeated everything. It's recovering from anxiety addiction. It's changing my neural wiring.

It's inviting Joy in. She's a more distant relative, but always happy to hear from me.

In remission

If my twin sisters used my anxiety for the planet to lure me into an addictive way of working, there's an important nuance. Heroin and the rest grab the ancient brain quick and are hard to shake. While they grip they harm. Despite Churchill's *bon mot* that he'd taken more out of alcohol than alcohol had taken out of him, his deep depressions suggest otherwise.

Churchill aside, the addictions squeeze the brain and harm the life. My way of working ran me down dangerously, it's true.

I'm now in remission from work on a beach in Mexico.

My way of working produced good though. It produced ClientEarth, the most effective legal group for the environment on the planet. It's taken me a long time to begin to see what a solid contribution that is.

Now in remission it's time to declare victory.

I can soften my approach to increase my longevity. Apply the local rule here, *poco a poco*. Appreciate my life. Write what I can. Contribute what I can. Invite Joy in. Go deeper.

LIFE RIPPED OPEN

What would life be like ripped open to reality, nothing to get in the way. Feet on ground, soles knowing Earth. Joy just joy, depression just depression, working to help the life of all life.

Scarlet tanager sings from a branch in sunlight.

Phone's vibrating

after Du Fu

photons cascade
flood my neural nets
from my electronic companions

brighter than I'm wired for
they compel
demand attention
gratify briefly
addict

so I remember
friendship offered by books
consolation delivered through silence
smiles conveyed by strangers
newly opened leaves bearing insect inscriptions

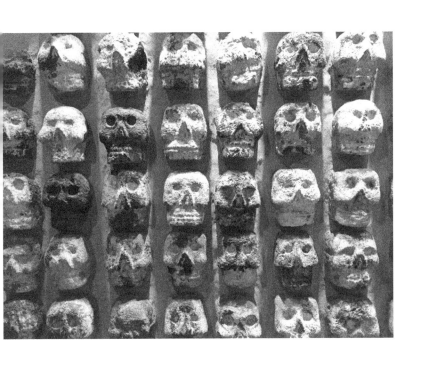

The Book of
Unapologetic Rest

Sabbatical onset

Time for a sabbatical. It starts in the Spanish seaside town of Sitges. Sleeping in the old town, I walk the front every morning. First impressions as I case the joint:

When last were clouds against blue close as breath, whistles of spotless starlings the music. Baggage down, find where feet take me.

Monk parakeets in palms along the front, loud and invasive and I love them. I don't need any more breakthroughs. I need to integrate my life.

Being gay is a mystery, like all good things.

Studying the hooks in my heart, I realize that when someone makes you hate them they own you.

Forest and sofa

From a notice to visitors at the most southerly ancient forest in Africa:

Sit on the benches along the forest trail. Absorb the scents of tree blossoms, earth, mosses and leaves. Look out for bushbuck grazing.

From curatorial notes at an exhibition of Black painters in Cape Town:

Lounging, hands locked behind our heads, relishing the peace that comes with being still, we rest, unwind and indulge...we are content in our recumbency. Fully reclined, sinking into soft plush sofas, limbs stretched out, we revel in idleness with no rush required....This is the dreamscape of slow wondrous living, of radical self-preservation...and of unapologetic rest.

Go deeper

Still fragile. My Zen teacher Maezumi comes again to mind. His last words to me were, "I want you to go deeper!" The time for going deeper is now. The question is how. I turn to advice from old master Hongzhi Zhengjeu:

Merge your mind with cosmic space.
Integrate your action with myriad forms.

This is his prescription for how to go deeper. *Merge,* he says. *Integrate*, he says. How to take his medicine? He gives no clues. Let me start this way:

Merge
When meditation's quiet, mind opens.

Integrate
When others anger me, turn a firehose of love on them to cool the flames.

Merge
A thought selects and magnifies a pixel of the Universe. Focusing like this narrows perception, feelings, consciousness. Open the aperture.

Integrate
Be grateful through the anxiety, pain, exhaustion.

Merge
Stop fixing things.

Integrate

When burnout comes accept its teachings.

Merge

Note the horizon. Add nothing.

Integrate

When hiking, offer your water to your companion before drinking.

Merge

When the fly walks on your face, that's just what it does.

Integrate

Swat the fly.

Untroubled by power

I'm now untroubled by power. It's let me go.

Today on a mountain in South Africa, I saw dung beetles roll their ball. Li Bai's reflection came back to me: if only people in the capital could appreciate what I have here.

Détente

If I don't interfere it works smoothly. If I manage it, what's spontaneous goes. Even worrying about breathing brings anxiety.

Listening to natural soundscapes opens doors.

If I want to engage in radical self-preservation, just trust.

Today I will

The question is how to inhabit my life now, how to re-inhabit it. There was always a driving purpose. It rode me too hard, wore out brain and bone.

The purpose remains. The question is how to play the notes more softly, penetrating yet softer. So today I will walk away from social media and the news. Enter the life world of a moth, a toad, a proteus. Feel how my body is aging in ways stress covered up.

Make plans for grand projects then let them go like clouds moving through big blue sky.

Leverage

Integrate

Returning to America, looking at the rightwing's power, its disdain of facts and denial of climate change. I wonder if western democracies can move fast enough to prevent the worst, or is a reality-based autocracy with democratic characteristics a better chance.

Looking at how I can do the most to slow down global heating I'm weighing an invitation to advise on greening China's global investments.

Maybe the way to spur America is for Americans to see China take the lead. Maybe this will light their competitive fuse. It worked with Sputnik.

Merge

Sometimes looking out at the sunlight is enough.

Dance

Needing a friend, I pick up Du Fu. He tells me:

Joy and sadness take turns
in a dance we don't control

So here's what I will do: build the dancefloor for Joy, set out the refreshments, tune and play the instruments.

There may be no controlling, but there's the power of invitation.

KOAN

My koan these decades

save civilization
save nature

solving it
I've thrown myself against the wall
again and again

sabbatical brings a new facet
saving myself

same koan

The Book of Simple Wants

A BASKET OF MELONS

What connection do melons have with enlightenment? I like
a story about a monk called Daito who lived in 13th century
Japan. Daito did his meditation and had an awakening. Then his
teacher died, and Daito could have gained power and prestige
by becoming the abbot of the temple.

That was not Daito's idea though. He ran away to Kyoto, where
he went into hiding. He lived with beggars under a bridge. He
wore rags, a coat made of reeds, had wild hair. The great thing
from his point of view was that he was free. No responsibility.
No having to be what other people wanted him to be.

He lived like this for twenty years, and all indications are he
would have liked to live the rest of his life this way.

But rumors started that there was a deeply enlightened Zen
monk living under a bridge as a beggar. Eventually the stories
reached the Palace. The Emperor put his secret service to work.
Apparently the hidden master was crazy about melons.

The Emperor hit on a stratagem. He disguised himself, and took a
basket of perfectly ripe melons. He went to the bridge, displayed the
melons and asked, "Can anyone come up and take a melon without
using his legs?" One of the beggars ran up and shouted, "Give it
to me without using your hands!" and then grabbed a melon.

The emperor had caught his man. The Emperor took Daito
back to the palace and made him give talks on Zen. This led

to building a major temple and eventually his being declared National Teacher.

There are times when we all want to go and hide. Each of us has their melon, though, the thing we love, the hook that the world will use to pull us back into circulation. And that's a good thing, like I hope it was for Daito.

Moon in blue

When I first looked up and saw the Moon in the sky in daytime I was shocked.

It seemed impossible to the small boy I was. It seemed wondrous. It seemed like a secret the Moon and I shared, the way it could show its face boldly in the middle of the day. Perhaps this secret was reserved for just a few devotees like me.

Yesterday I saw the Moon three quarters full in a bright blue sky, hiding from time to time behind palm trees as I walked down the street.

A hazy Moon is praised in Asian poetry. For me, it's the pale Moon in blue sky in daylight. That's the Moon for me.

I never go looking for it. Yet it always finds me. When it does, it still subtly subverts everything.

Textures

Colors and sounds are not digital, with sharp jumps between them. They're analogue, with transitions so subtle as to approach the infinite. We know that about sounds and colors, but textures are like this too. Textures reward attention.

The feeling on the soles of bare feet in the summer as we walk across the parking lot then across the sand.

The softness of a baby's skin, the scratch of a cat's tongue, the resistance of an onion as you chop it.

The grit of the soil as you plunge in the trowel to place the plant, when the soil's dry, when it's wet.

Textures every day are a fleeting communion with realities we don't control but can be informed by.

Listening

Pretending to listen is easy. We look at the person, refrain from speaking. It looks like listening.

When our mind is teeming, though, even if we try to listen, the swarm of thoughts clouds our attention, so we are just pretending.

To listen the mind needs to be silent. Then the voice of the other, the intention of the other, carries through as if our mind were a cathedral resonating to their voice.

It's frustrating, pretending to listen. It can be agitating to oneself, and the other.

Listening like a cathedral is really listening, and is satisfying.

Of course, if the other is difficult, their resonance becomes dissonance. You can always close the cathedral's great doors, walk away, the cathedral unsullied.

Assuming you do want to keep listening, then when it's time to talk, you just talk.

Food and choices

Simple food wraps us in its sincerity.

Tea is a plant medicine we welcome in.

One of my most famous friends wears blue jeans and black tee shirts every day.

Some of my friends live for long bike rides, or making and listening to music, or making food to share with others, or visiting with a few old friends.

Adversity will come. When it comes it will always be experienced as adversity. Adversity is just adversity. Simple things, though, retain value.

Intimates

We co-evolved with just two species: dogs and horses. That's what biologists say. Dogs and horses lived and worked alongside us from before time. Their genes and dispositions tailored themselves toward ours and ours toward them. Our hearts open easily to them and we think of them as someone we can have a relationship with, part of the family.

In a less mutually regarding way, we evolved with all living things. When we encounter these, their wildness gives us life.

Before there were motors, the sound of the world was made by wind and birdsong.

Birds remain innately wild. Stare into their dinosaur eyes. Great clarity and attention are returned, but the emotion is hard to read. Their lips are hard and so we don't know what a bird smile looks like.

Encounters with birds open us always, whether an eagle soaring above a peak or a sparrow hunting crumbs. The sparrow is as wild and remarkable and deserving of attention as the eagle.

If you find yourself in a natural place and wait for the birds, they come. Standing still you are able, if not to read their feelings in their faces, nevertheless to enter into their world. How that pair of tits take turns flying off to find caterpillars for their nestlings. We sense how hard they are working, how their focused attention mirrors that we give our children. We get to share a mind space with them and feel for them.

The voice of the world expresses itself in birdsong still.

It is not hard to hear or enter into.

Sunlight

The revelation that we are made of stardust is now widely shared. So let's open the windows of thoughts and let in the sunlight.

We are made of sunlight as much as of stardust. The sunlight is what animates the dust.

The exceptions are the strange anatomies living off chemicals that pour out of boiling hot springs deep on the ocean floor. There is talk that life evolved down there, but if so it moved to a different diet as it migrated miles up to catch the sunlight.

Plants are the shamans who feed us and everyone we eat. They take sunlight and water and carbon dioxide and make coffee, bacon and eggs. We eat sunlight at every meal. Even mushrooms grown in the dark eat the remains of things that ate sunlight.

Since we are made from it, we have an affinity for sunlight. We all can recall moments when sunlight was a gift.

Here are two. One morning when clouds parted over the North Sea, and sunlight turned the surface of the sea into a field of broken mirrors. Another when, in a depressed neighborhood of New York, sunbeams fell down through the elevated railroad tracks and gilded whatever they touched.

Savoring the endless flavors of sunlight takes a lifetime.

Snails can't laugh

When I hear my husband from a distance meeting someone new, they always laugh together in the first few minutes.

Snails must have another way of making friends, but for us laughter will do it. When I talk to a group, even about avoiding the end of civilization, I always get them laughing a few times to build rapport.

The writer Norman Cousins said he cured a fatal illness by watching films that made him belly laugh until he was well again.

Laughter can be provoked like a spark from flint by banging unexpected things together. Comedians do it all the time.

My current favorite joke is from Groucho Marx: Time flies like an arrow. Fruit flies like a banana.

He was a laughter provocateur. But laughter can be provoked by the clash of unexpected ideas or circumstances in the kitchen, classroom, bedroom. Everyplace is a good place to laugh.

Wanting a laugh, that's not a hard itch to scratch.

And a good laugh redeems a day.

Final thoughts

At the end of life, when people are asked what they wish they'd done differently, or more of, the answer is consistent.

I wish I'd spent more time with loved ones, they say. I wish I'd had more time with family and friends. I wish I hadn't let work take so much of my time and energy away from loving relationships. That's what I wish I'd done differently.

No one ever wishes they'd worked more.

Wanting the warmth, that's what they say is important. Imagine if they'd gone into that warmth and basked in it as much as they wanted.

Simple wants make a happy life.

From the shore

after Li He

see the whales
        in the bay

who sieve its waters
        and do as they please

The Book of Things
I Need to Remember

No one

No one ever woke up and wished they'd drunk more the night before. No one ever surfaced from the sea and resented the sky. No one ever met the queen and forgot. No one ever lost the right to be present. No one ever met a honeybee and failed to be improved. No one ever turned his hand against another unjustly without reducing his own world. No one ever forgot the first time they fell in love. No one ever loved and felt no pain. No one in love ever regretted being alive. No one dead ever regretted living.

Same river

Greek gods still make appearances in poems but I prefer people with glints of deep reaches. Whose vision penetrates scattering surfaces to glimpse what's at the bottom.

Imagine walking thyme and rosemary hills, falling in love with Reason before anyone else wooed her. Pre-Socratic philosophers did this and were my early favorites. Parmenides taught me that everything interconnects into a single unity forever unchanging. Reality enjoys timelessness while the data of the senses is superficial to the point of illusion. Walking the hills of Elea this is what he learned.

Zeno his student and *reductio* master supplied supporting paradoxes: subdivide distance toward infinity and Achilles can't outrun the tortoise nor the arrow fly. Motion too is illusion he said to make the point.

The work of such masters filled me early and became my refuge and delight. I imagined a universe where what they said is true. Lived inside and studied it.

The foundations of common sense can be subverted to seek a place of deeper meaning. Quiet exploration of counterfactuality became the rebelliousness of my teen years, liberating, cloaking, recalibrating, opening ways to insight.

Seeing through illusions others want to bind you with opens the eyes. See through illusions they do not see are binding them and you walk free.

Heraclitus looked beyond scattering surfaces from another vantage then declaimed everything is flux. All change all the time ceaselessly. You can't step in the same river twice he said. We can take it further: you can't step in the *same* river once.

The opposite of a test

Why are you alive. Today. Dogs and cauliflowers don't need to answer but you do. I do. Every morning. Why are you alive. You could lie down like a small mammal on the forest floor and go. Gaining release.

Only a few among the world's great number would care. Then the ripples of caring would close. All of us are like this. Even a star burns out its fuel. So why are you alive. Why are you here today. This is the opposite of a test.

Still

We can still eat oranges. We can still walk on sand. We can still feel water receding to pull sand from under our feet. We can still feel our hands as we wash our face. We can still feel the hand that shakes ours. We can still hand our ticket to the conductor on the train. We can still train ourselves to play the piano or speak French. We can still play poker or play dumb. We can still dumb down our idea to make the other comfortable. We can still feel comfortable in a suit or dress. We can still dress for the occasion.

We can still forget to be kind. We can still kind of hope to do better next time. We can still time our responses to make the other feel listened to. We can still listen to what the other has to say in the hope to connect. We can still hope to find the perfect partner. We can still partner with the best we can find. We can still find we need to build another nest.

We can still bother. We can still try. We can still count our breaths as we lie in the dark and seek illumination.

Perfectionist

There was a man down the street called Charlie, from the house I lived in till I was five. The houses on the block had small lawns and backyards always neat. All except Charlie's. Charlie was a perfectionist. My father, in his late thirties then, took maybe an hour on the weekend to cut grass front and back with a hand mower whenever it was needed. Not Charlie. Perfection required time and he was a busy man.

So he let his yard grow into a suburban jungle until he had a whole day to do it to his perfect satisfaction. He would end his ministrations by taking out nail scissors, kneeling down from every edge and angle to see if an errant blade of grass survived and if so trim it. Charlie would call over my father to admire the perfection he achieved by this method. My father would politely tell him it looked like a putting green. Then come home to marvel at how Charlie could live with a mess most of the time then have a perfect result that would last for a few hours or days.

That perfect result was a particular annoyance to my father. He would say of the nail scissor trimming, who's going to see it from Times Square!

No cloud

No one finds their way without wandering. No democracy is secured by the checks and balances of its constitution alone. No one knows what is beyond death. No cloud lasts forever. No flower opens without willing to be pollinated.

Un

Unexamined, a life not worth living; unwilling, not rising to the present occasion; unrepentant, unable to form authentic relationships; unseeing, what happens if you let the culture set your norms; unfaithful, living by ideology; unwitting, not knowing mortality; unfocused, letting external voices overcome internal quiet; unwelcome, reality seen from inside shadow; unmitigated, the disaster of our present direction.

Unattached, able to see clearly; unremitting, the effort it takes; unwavering, and life is flowing; unadorned, able to be seen; unknowable, the future; unreachable, the past; unafraid, the present in its natural disposition; unabated, the Sun rising in the morning; unarmed, on the side of life; unborn, depending on our wisdom; unbounded, the possible futures; unopposed, when we turn to face ourselves; unassailable, our capacity.

DECISIONS IN A TYPHOON

In the middle of the Pacific in WWII, my father's warship was overtaken by a typhoon. Responsible for a large crew of men, he faced day after day of extreme danger. In a maelstrom he had to make decisions their lives depended on.

He told me he struggled to make sure he'd taken everything into account in each decision. What was most important though was to act, to actually decide. When you have an entire ship's crew looking up to you, he said, the men need decisive action. More important than getting it right is making a decision.

To do list

Go deeper into the nature of reality. Be more loving.
Write better essays and more of them.
Be more strategic about protecting Nature.
Understand how AI will make millions jobless.
Understand how climate change will make hundreds of
    millions migrate.
Figure out something practical to do about it.
Practice scales before playing partitas.

Einstein's belt

A man of my type, Einstein said, needs a belt to hold up his pants.
When I read this in college I cried 'who else is a man of *his* type!'

It didn't occur to me he wasn't talking physics.

Now I'm the age when he talked trousers, I keep tightening my
belt so my pants don't fall down.

What you do

It's not what you do but what you leave undone. Did I fail when she needed it, to say her work had value. When insecurity flecked his eye, did I extend hope's hand. Could I hear through my grievance what they meant to say.

On a local scale, the irascible, the annoyed, the difficult. They offer opportunities to strengthen my kindness muscles.

On a global scale, the strongmen, the malevolent, the Earth slayers. They offer opportunities for strategic action.

Do I recall each day that my job is to love everyone whose feet, like mine, are held down by gravity. To support their right action, to offer correction when needed.

To give voice to what is commonly experienced but seldom expressed.

Taking care of this donkey I ride through the day.

Protecting our family

We share the same Mother, so we're all sisters and brothers.

We need to work together to protect the Family and the family Home.

It's simple but not easy.

To fall asleep

What I tell myself to fall asleep:

Sharks are still left in the sea, ten percent of them, so we can save the rest.

There is more intelligent life on Earth than ever before.

We know how to reduce global heating.

The future is ours to fight for, and win.

Octopus and me

the octopus is dreaming
twitches and rapid eye movements

what is the octopus dreaming of?
crabs and fish

what am I dreaming of?
oceans unharmed

octopus and me
different pillows

same dream

Endnotes

In a fog I met a man: This essay was inspired by walking through Olafur Eliasson's fog sculpture in the 2020 Tate Modern's show of his work.

Over tea: The quotation is from: *Nagarjuna's "Seventy Stanzas",* by David Ross Komito, p. 35 (Snow Lion 1987).

Next day's cup: Id. at 41.

Rules of the game: This essay was inspired by the book review: The Thinker's Thinker, by Anthony Gottlieb, New Yorker, 4 May 2020, reviewing *Frank Ramsey: A Sheer Excess of Powers* (Oxford), by Cheryl Misak. The final line of the essay incorporates language from the review.

Strange attractor: This essay was inspired by a conversation I had with a professor at Berkeley in the early 1990s. I've never forgotten her, though I can no longer recall her name or find her work online.

Complexity: The quotation is from *Human Compatible: Artificial Intelligence and the Problem of Control*, by Stuart Russell, p. 39 (Viking 2019).

Burning: the right-hand stanza of this poem was inspired by a New Scientist article I admired but can no longer track down.

Acknowledgments

In a real way, everyone I have met or read throughout my life has contributed to this book, and I thank them. Some, though, need singling out.

The Wale family for giving us refuge in nature while I was working on this book. Caitlin Wale heard our need for a remote place to start my sabbatical, and her family offered their house in Infanta, South Africa, sixty miles down a dirt road, where the southern right whales breed offshore, just beyond the deck. A Cape rock thrush visited in the morning, a Cape robin-chat popped into the house to check on how my manuscript was progressing, and of course there were those right whales.

Antony Osler, the Wale family's Zen teacher, offered inspiration through his book *Stoep Zen,* and his solid practice in the Karoo. He then went beyond and also gave editorial advice and encouragement of a deep and sensitive kind, rejigged the title of the book, and offered good words of endorsement for the cover.

I'm grateful to Ben Goldsmith, Roshi Joan Halifax, Arianna Huffington and Gabrielle Walker, for each taking time to read, consider, and reflect on the manuscript, and offer words of encouragement to other readers for the book's cover.

My beta readers Richard Erickson, Caitlin Wale, Susan Weiner and Carol Wishcamper each approached the manuscript with an open heart and a sharp pencil, and I'm grateful for their encouragement and help in finalizing the manuscript.

I bow to Martin Goodman, who called the book into being. He went on to suggest that this should be a book of essays not poems. He also had the deepest editorial hand, as always, in shaping the book. Without him it would not exist.

Printed in the USA
CPSIA information can be obtained
at www.ICGtesting.com
JSHW012041250324
59902JS00001B/1